MESSAGE OF BIBLICAL SPIRITUALITY
Editorial Director: Carolyn Osiek, RSCJ

Volume 14

The Catholic Epistles
&
Hebrews

Rea McDonnell, SSND

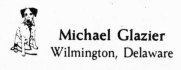

Michael Glazier
Wilmington, Delaware

About the Author

REA McDONNELL, SSND, directs continuing education at the Washington Theological Union where she is assistant professor. She simultaneously teaches biblical spirituality in graduate programs for pastoral counseling at Emmanuel College, Boston and Loyola College of Maryland.

First published in 1986 by Michael Glazier, Inc. 1935 West Fourth Street, Wilmington, Delaware, 19805. ©1986 by Michael Glazier, Inc. All rights reserved. Library of Congress Catalog Card Number: 85-45559. International Standard Book Numbers: *Message of Biblical Spirituality* series: 0-89453-550-1, cloth; 0-89453-566-8, paper. THE CATHOLIC EPISTLES: 0-89453-564-1, cloth; 0-89453-580-3, paper. Typography by Dick Smith, Connie Runkel. Cover design by Florence Bern. Printed in the United States of America.

TABLE OF CONTENTS

EDITOR'S PREFACE

One of the characteristics of church life today is a revived interest in spirituality. There is a growing list of resources in this area, yet the need for more is not exhausted. People are yearning for guidance in living an integrated life of faith in which belief, attitude, affections, prayer, and action form a cohesive unity which gives meaning to their lives.

The biblical tradition is a rich resource for the variety of ways in which people have heard God's call to live a life of faith and fidelity. In each of the biblical books we have a witness to the initiative of God in human history and to the attempts of people not so different from ourselves to respond to the revelation of God's love and care.

The fifteen volumes in the *Message of Biblical Spirituality* series aim to provide ready access to the treasury of biblical faith. Modern social science has made us aware of how the particular way in which one views reality conditions the ways in which one will interpret experience and life itself. Each volume in this series is an attempt to retell and interpret the biblical story from within the faith perspective that originally formed it. Each seeks to portray what it is like to see God, the world, and oneself from a particular point of view and to search for ways to respond faithfully to that vision. We who are citizens of our twentieth century world cannot be people of the ancient biblical world, but we can grow closer to their experience and their faith and thus closer to God, through the living Word of God which is the Bible.

The series includes an international group of authors representing England, Ireland, Canada, and the United States, but whose life experience has included first-hand knowledge of many other countries. All are proven scholars and committed believers whose faith is as important to them as their scholarship. Each acts as interpreter of one part of the biblical tradition in order to enable its spiritual vitality to be passed on to others. It is our hope that through their labor the reader will be able to enter more deeply into the life of faith, hope, and love through a fuller understanding of and appreciation for the biblical Word as handed down to us by God's faithful witnesses, the biblical authors themselves.

Carolyn Osiek, RSCJ
Associate Professor of New Testament Studies
Catholic Theological Union, Chicago

ACKNOWLEDGEMENTS

Thanks to Rachel Callahan, CSC, Nancy Steckel, and Carol Ann Smith, SHCJ, who were with me as I wrote these chapters. They have helped me live more deeply and freely, and I am grateful.

Thanks to my secretary, Janet Sidor, who with grace and efficiency, handled all the details of a busy continuing education office while I was on sabbatical, and to the Washington Theological Union for the time to write. Thanks to Norrine and Lou Migliorini for lending me their oceanfront condo for writing and feeding gulls.

Rea McDonnell, SSND
Pentecost, 1986

INTRODUCTION

Snow covered the Maryland Shore. The gulls were hungry, so I braved the winter's fierce wind to throw them bread from my balcony. They tried to fly to me and again and again the wind blew them up and away from the food. Couldn't the building protect them from the wind if only they would fly a little lower? I wondered. On and on they came, only to be buffeted away. If only they would walk to me. I shook my head in disappointment, and, too numbed with cold to hold out my goodies for them any longer, returned to the warmth.

Spirituality is meant to make us soar, like gulls, straight to God for nourishment. The winds of the world and the cold keep discouraging us in our flight to God. Like my building, the church has tried to protect us from the wind over the centuries but most of us don't like to fly low. Walking to God? Out of the question!

There is a tale of a man who wanted to reach God and so climbed the highest mountain under all kinds of difficulty only to discover emptiness. He returned discouraged to the base of the mountain, and there to his surprise, was God. God told him: "While you were so busy struggling up the mountain to find me, you didn't see me coming down the mountain to be with you."

Biblical spirituality is an incarnational spirituality, one in which God comes to us, takes flesh in our lives, helps us discover life and love and mystery in the midst of our day-to-day joys, sorrows, and blahs. Biblical spirituality is a way to walk to God who wants to nourish us, and who never turns away, numbed by cold. The editor of this series has developed an excellent comprehensive description of biblical spirituality. By biblical spirituality I will simply mean: our response to God who comes to us, our relationship with God.

Together, we begin our search to discover that spirituality which formed and fostered the five different communities which produced *James, I and II Peter, Jude* and *Hebrews.* As you know from your own experience, the spirituality of each person, each family, each community, each parish is unique. Thus, I must treat each of these five "epistles" individually.

Rather than simply comment on the spirituality operative in the first century communities which produced *James, I and II Peter, Jude,* and *Hebrews,* however, I invite you, my readers, to articulate your own twentieth century spirituality. I invite you to share with others in your current community, and then to put your personal and communal spirituality in dialogue with that of your first century brothers and sisters. By your current community I mean your family or religious community, your support group or prayer group, your liturgical committee or, perhaps, even a new group called together by you to pray with and dicuss these biblical writings. There are not many commentaries on these particular writings and so you and your group may break new ground in savoring their message. Even the variety of translations which your group will undoubtedly use will enrich your understanding of passages. Do not be afraid to question these ancient texts, but try to let the texts question you and challenge you to new depths in your relationship with God.

That is why I write and you read: that we may be led to new depths in our relationship with God. To work with Scripture — reading, studying, sharing — is to worship.

We are invited to digest the Word of God, not only with our minds but with all our human faculties: mind, will, memory, imagination, emotions (summed up in the language of Jewish spirituality as "the heart"). To digest the Word of God is as graced an activity as digesting holy communion. Scripture is a sacrament, an outward sign, given us by God, that we might be graced to know, love and live God more completely in service of God's people.[1]

Scripture is a privileged way to encounter God, in the New Testament, to encounter Christ, the risen Lord, who continues to teach us and motivate us through the Spirit. Thus, we come to each of these five "epistles" asking the Spirit to open us to whatever Christ wants us to know about himself, ourselves, and our community which is the church. We ask the Spirit as we study, reflect on, share each particular passage to help us respond to the risen Lord as whole-heartedly as we can.

Let us begin our pilgrimage into the spiritual life of these early communities first by remembering our own spiritual life, our relationship with God: its birth, growth, highlights, low

---

[1]Rea McDonnell, SSND, *Prayer Pilgrimage Through Scripture*, New York: Paulist, 1984, pp. 8-10.

points. After reflecting on these questions in the presence of
the Lord (be that God, Jesus, or the Spirit), share your
responses with a friend, a spouse, a group. This is not a time for
correcting or being corrected, not a time to discuss "truth," let
alone judge. Your responses to these questions are your own
unique truth in your own unique relationship with God.
Thus, the sharing of responses calls for a listening, respectful
partner or group who need not make any verbal response at
all.

● Of all your relationships, which are most meaningful to
you? Why?

● Besides relationships, where do you find meaning in
your life?

● Remember and savor some moments (days, years) in
your life when you felt free. Be as concrete as possible in your
memories. When you felt happy . . . When you felt close to
God (Jesus, Spirit). . .

● What principle(s) do you live by? How did they come
to be part of you?

● Are you "a believer"? If so, in what? In whom? How
did that happen to you?

● What three or four experiences of the past year created
a sense of awe in you?

● What do you desire from life?

These questions may take days or weeks to ponder. You
may not be able to race through this little volume. Yet I do not

invite you to learn *about* the spiritualities of these biblical authors and their communities. I invite you to participate in them, to try them on for size, for meaningfulness in your own Christian life. To help you in that process, I will suggest short sections of these epistles for your reading, reflecting and praying; I will also break in to my commentary with questions about your own experience so that you may better put your experience in dialogue with these first century Christians. Finally, I invite you to "taste and see the goodness of the Lord" (Ps 34:8) as the Spirit reveals God, Jesus and ourselves in these biblical writings.

JAMES

JAMES

●Much of *James* will be devoted to moral exhortation. How do you describe morality? Who/what has shaped your morality through the years? Can you remember concretely certain incidents?

●This author spells out the relationship between faith and good works. What does faith mean to you? How does it operate in your life? Thank God for your faith and ask for a deepening of it.

●How would you describe wisdom? What women and men whom you know do you consider wise? Concretely, what qualities do you find in a wise person? Thank God for gifting you with wisdom (a gift of the Spirit given in baptism) and ask for a deepening of it.

Introduction

The origins and author of the epistle of James are obscure. Both ancient and modern scholars have disputed the nature, purpose, and readership of what is better called a homily than an epistle or letter. Although it begins like a letter, there is no conclusion which marks it as a letter. Nor is it written to any specific community and thus, *James* is called "catholic" or universal, that is, directed to any or all Christian communities.

A homily is a piece of moral exhortation. Unlike a Christian sermon which also would include a proclamation of God's goodness or Jesus' love or some "good news" to which the hearers are then exhorted to respond, this text moves immediately into a call for the readers' moral response. Indeed, the author refers so seldom to Jesus that some commentators have thought perhaps a Jewish-Christian teacher merely "baptized" a Jewish homily by inserting the name of Jesus Christ in 1:1 (chapter 1, verse 1) and 2:1.

There is general agreement that *James* is a homily, useful primarily for Jewish-Christians. There is general disagreement over the possibility of its origins as a Jewish document, its author and its date. *James* opens with a greeting to the "Twelve Tribes in the Diaspora," a reference to the gathering of Jewish communities in cities outside the homeland. If it were originally a Jewish writing, it could be addressed to those communities. If it is indeed of Christian origins, the author could be writing to the "new Israel" as some New Testament authors understood the young Christian church, made up in most cities of converts from Judaism and paganism.

The author, James, describes himself as "a servant of God and of the Lord Jesus Christ." That self-designation does not point to James, one of the Twelve and son of Zebedee; nor to James, son of Alphaeus, sometimes called "The Less," another of the Twelve, nor to James, "brother of the Lord," not one of the Twelve but leader of the young Christian church in

Jerusalem who died about 62 AD. Much discussion has centered on dating the epistle from the dates of these men, but our James could be another teacher, thoroughly unconnected with the other three.

James would have been born of the Jewish race and steeped in the language of the Hebrew scriptures translated into Greek, the Septuagint (LXX, for Seventy, named after the seventy legendary Jewish scholars who made the translation). James' Greek, obviously his mother tongue, is among the most perfect and literary in all the New Testament writings. Literary and rhetorical devices indicate James' advanced learning and talent. Many allusions to the Jewish scriptures and to the gospel sayings point to his contemplative assimilation of both a Jewish and a Christian spirituality. Wisdom literature in particular has influenced his world view, and may even be the reason his moral imperatives seem strung together like the maxims of Jewish wisdom.

Some scholars want to attribute *James* to James of Jerusalem and thus date it before 62 AD. Some claim that the kind of Jewish Christianity which James addresses did not exist after the fall of Jerusalem in 70 AD, but since this homily is addressed universally to Christian communities in far-flung cities of the Empire, the fall of Jerusalem is not a factor. *James* seems to be more contemporary with the gospel of Matthew and the Pastoral Epistles. With Richard Kugelman, CP,[1] I would hold that *James* was written in the last decades of the first century.

Our final question of introduction is whether *James* origi-

[1]Richard Kugelman, CP, *James and Jude*, New Testament Message, Wilmington, DE: Michael Glazier, Inc., 1980.

nated in a Christian community or whether a Christian teacher added a few references to Jesus Christ so that the homily might be applicable to Christians, particularly if they were converts from Judaism. With Kugelman I hold that this is a Christian composition, but for different reasons. He concludes that the hope of Christ's return (eschatology) and the "law of liberty" (Ja 1:25, 2:12) as gospel indicate Christian origins.[2] There is nothing, however, which designates the *parousia* (Greek word for arrival or presence) as the coming of Christ; it could refer to the Jewish apocalyptic hope of God's own coming with justice for the nations. Nor does the text equate the "law of liberty" with the gospel. Indeed the "royal law" of 2:8 is specifically the great commandment of the Jews: love your neighbor as yourselves.[3] One verse in that chapter, however, could point to Jewish origins. To assign guilt for the "whole law" (2:10) for a single transgression is similar to rabbinical teaching.[4]

On the other hand, the name of "the Lord" and James' own gospel orientation point to a homily Christian in origin. "The name by which you are called" or "the honorable name which was invoked over you" (2:7) can express the early church's devotion to the name of Jesus. According to other New Testament (from now on, NT) books, the name of Jesus had power to heal; converts were baptized in that name; and in *James*, the sick were anointed "in the name of the Lord"

[2]*Ibid*, p. 9.

[3]*Ibid*, pp. 23-27.

[4]*Ibid*, p. 22.

(5:14). It would be expected that healing, one of the gifts of the Spirit operating in the young church, would be associated with the powerful name of Jesus, the Lord. In the same section on anointing, the elders of the Christian *ecclesia* (Greek for church) were to anoint. Jewish elders were teachers; we have no records of their care for the sick nor of any anointing rites in Judaism at that time.

Most significant in our detective work, however, is the way in which James is steeped in gospel tradition. So much of his homily is based on allusions to the gospel that either he, Jesus and the evangelists shared a common store of Jewish exhortation, or James has meditated often and deeply on the oral and/or written gospel, particularly Matthew's, the work of a Jewish-Christian community. I opt for the latter.

If you really want to share the fruit of James' contemplation of the gospel of Jesus Christ, if you really want to share the spirituality of James and his community, you will have to open your NT and become involved with the Word of God to us through James. If you will let the Word of God address you personally then you need to read the scripture directly, carefully, prayerfully. To let the Word of God come to you directly will mean change in your life. Like rain or snow the Word comes, penetrating the earth, writes Isaiah (chapter 55), accomplishing that for which God sent it. Through James' homily, God sends us an invitation to grow and change and be deepened in all our relationships. I select three major themes in *James*, each of them an aspect of a biblical spirituality: 1) God takes the initiative in our relationship and we receive all from God; 2) we are not just individuals in relationship with God but a community; and 3) biblical faith flows into action.

God's Initiative and Our Receptivity

If James were the leader of the Jerusalem church or one of the Twelve, we would not know it from his simple self-designation: servant (*doulos* can also mean slave). He seems to practice what he preaches in his homily about humility, meekness, wisdom, receptivity to God. As he advocates for his readers, James is single-minded and speaks the truth authentically. Let us listen to him directly.

1:2-8

> ²Consider it all joy, my brothers and sisters, whenever you experience various trials, ³knowing that the testing of your faith works toward endurance. ⁴Let your endurance become perfect so that you may be complete and whole, wanting nothing. ⁵If any of you wants wisdom, ask God who gives to everyone without reserve, without reproach and wisdom will be given to you. ⁶But ask in faith. Do not doubt. The one who doubts is like a wave of the sea which is tossed and driven by the wind. ⁷,⁸Do not expect that a person who is double-minded, unstable in every way, will receive anything from the Lord.

Read out loud, slowly, the above verses. What do you notice? (If your translation uses the term "man" or "men," the Greek word *anthropos* means "human being"; please make that more accurate translation mentally; or when you read in public, feel free to substitute "human" or "person".)

In v. 3 James writes that a faith which is tested produces steadfastness (literally patience), a word used often in NT writings of this later period. Faith, that is, commitment to Jesus Christ, was severely tested by persecutions, sometimes physical persecution by the Romans, often emotional persecution and ostracism by Jews. James first wants to encourage his readers to joy and a humble, ready-even-to-suffer waiting on the Lord, which is the meaning of patience. In v. 5 he advocates a receptivity to God's gift of wisdom which is also closely allied with patience, a receiving from God rather than a manipulating or an imposing our ego on reality. The word in v. 6 for "without doubting" is used elsewhere in the NT to mean "discerning." One who waits for God is not only joyful, patient, wise but also discerning. Instead of being "double-minded" or "double-souled," (the only time *di/psychos* is used in the NT) there is a single-heartedness in the wise discerner, James writes in verses 7-8. The single-hearted can count on receiving all from the Lord.

1:9-18

⁹Let the humble brother or sister boast about their exaltation. ¹⁰Let the rich boast about their humiliation, for, like a flower of the field, they will pass away. ¹¹The sun rose with a hot wind and dried the grass. The flower fell and its beauty failed. Thus, will the rich fade away in their pursuits.

¹²Blessed is the one who endures trial. When such a person has been proved, he or she will receive the crown of life promised to those who love God. ¹³Let no one say when tempted, I am tested by God, because God is untempted by evil and tempts no one. ¹⁴It is our own desires, luring and enticing us, which are the temptation. ¹⁵Desire conceives and bears sin, and sin, when fully formed, brings forth death. ¹⁶Make no mistake, my beloved brothers and sisters. ¹⁷Every good and perfect gift from above comes from the father of lights in whom there is no shadow, only faithfulness. ¹⁸Freely, God brought us forth by a word of truth so that we should be the first fruits of all God's creatures.

Please read these verses slowly. What do they mean to you? One of the often-used gospel images to encourage simplicity of life is the lilies of the field. James reminds us of our dependence on God in successes and failures, our contingency frail as flowers (vv. 9-11).

A discerning and single-hearted person knows his or her own desires and motivations. Desire is a gift from God. In vv. 12-15, the word "desire," however, literally means lusts: inordinate, ungodly, grasping desire ("Lust" is used in some translations). Those lusts — for riches, power, success — lead to sin, and sin to death. On the other hand, in letting the Lord direct one's life, one can expect trials which lead to patience, and patience to the crown of life.

"Blessed" is the one who is tried (v. 12). To be blessed in Jewish tradition is to receive all that the blessing-one has to give. When the patriarch Isaac blessed his son Jacob there was nothing left of Isaac for Esau. When God blesses us, God pours out God's whole self. The crown of life is God's own life. No wonder *every* good, *every* perfect gift comes from the God who is like a father (v. 17). God has given us all of God's own life. Like a mother, God shares all life and gives us birth through a "word of truth."

1:19-25

¹⁹Know this, my beloved brothers and sisters. Let everyone be quick to hear, slow to speak, slow to anger. ²⁰Our anger does not work for the justice of God. ²¹Put aside all filth and excess of evil. In meekness receive the word deeply planted within you, a word powerful to save you. ²²Become doers of the word and not just hearers, deceiving yourselves. ²³If anyone hears the word and does not act on it, such a person is like someone who looks into a mirror. ²⁴Once having seen and then moved on, the person immediately forgets the image in the mirror. ²⁵Some

people look into the perfect law of freedom and continue faithfully. They are not hearers who forget, but doers who act. Such people will be blessed in their action.

Truth is an important aspect of the simplicity of life to which James urges us. For the Greek mind, truth had to do with a right understanding of reality. For the Jew, truth especially meant being true, faithful in relationships. We grow in truth through hearing, hearing and appropriating God's understanding of reality, hearing God's faithful love, and responding with our own fidelity in relationships. God speaks and gives birth to us in a "word of truth." We are challenged to respond, "quick to hear, slow to speak" (v. 19). That is an age-old maxim for appearing wise. Real wisdom, James would assure us, comes from our continued openness to hear, see, touch, taste God in our daily experiences. James would have us foster a contemplative, discerning attitude toward our lives. That would mean reflecting on the truth of them and the inauthenticity in them, on the fidelity and the infidelity which grow together in the human heart. "Receive with meekness the word planted in you, full of power to ' whole ' your souls/hearts" (*psychos* v. 21).

How to escape the *di/psychos,* the double-heartedness, which complicates and confuses our lives? James answers: Hear the word, let it take deeper and deeper root in you. God's word is "strong to save." The word "save" will return in *James* in the context of healing (5:15), as it often appears in the gospel ("Your faith has saved you."). Underlying the word "save" is the Hebrew *shalom* which means a saving, healing, peace-bringing, whole-making blessing of God.

To hear God's word of truth, calling us to single-heartedness, and not to act on it means self-deception (v. 22).

Throughout his homily James will return to this gospel theme about the interaction of hearing God and acting on what we hear: "Not everyone who says, 'Lord, Lord . . .'" This is what James urges: if it is God's word we hear, action can flow from us easily, simply — not in grandiose projects and schemes for kingdom-building, but in our alert response to the voice of God in whomever, whatever we encounter moment by moment. That ease and simplicity of action is the liberty, the freedom which is so natural that James can call it a perfect law (1:25 and 2:12). What is this perfect law? It is like a mirror.

We look into the word of God as into a mirror. Some scholars equate that word/law with the Jewish Law or with the gospel (Kugelman, p. 22). The Word, the correcting mirror of ourselves, into whom we look is Jesus himself. To see ourselves in Jesus is to be made whole, set free.

This law of freedom, then, is a law to which eventually we do not even advert because, in Christ, we experience a kind of co-naturality with God. God expresses a continuing word of love and desire and our moment-to-moment response in action is our spirituality as well as our morality. It is our truth.

1:26

> If you consider yourself religious, yet do not curb your tongue, you deceive your own heart and your religion is empty.

3:1-10

> **3** Be careful of becoming teachers, my brothers and sisters, because you know that teachers are more likely to be judged. [2]In many ways we all stumble. If someone does not make mistakes in speech, such a person is perfect and able to control the entire

self. ³We put bridles into the mouths of horses to make them obey us; we thus can direct their whole bodies. ⁴Large ships too, when driven by strong winds, are directed by a tiny rudder wherever the pilot decides. ⁵So too the tongue. It is so small and yet boasts great things. Notice too how a little fire kindles a great forest. ⁶The tongue is a fire . . . ⁸which no human being can tame. It is an unruly evil, full of deadly poison. ⁹With the tongue we bless the Lord and Father; with it we curse human beings who are in the image of God. ¹⁰From the same mouth comes blessing and cursing. This is not right, my brothers and sisters.

Please read these verses, remembering as specifically as you can your experience of the power of your own and others' tongues. James is a teacher (3:1). As a man steeped in a biblical spirituality he undoubtedly often meditated on *Isaiah* and the power of the gifts God had given him:

The Lord God has given me the tongue of a teacher and skill to console the weary with a word in the morning; God sharpened my hearing that I might listen like one who is taught.
(Is 50:4 NEB)

James is writing at a time when unorthodox Christian teachers (perhaps super-apostles, boasting miracle-workers like Paul's opponents in Corinth; cf II Cor 11-12) were confusing new Christians. Not only was James concerned about the possible intellectual confusion of these young Christian churches; he also must have realized how easily communities broke into factions (cf Corinthian letters, Philippians, Clement). "If you have bitter jealousy and rivalry in your heart, do not boast and lie against the truth" (3:14). God's gift of the tongue, given to comfort and to bless God (3:9), can be misused.

James 4:1-10

4 What causes conflicts and fighting among you? Is it not that your bodily lusts are at war within you? ²You want something and cannot get it and so you kill. You covet and cannot obtain what you want so you fight and quarrel. ³You don't get what you want because you don't ask for it — or if you do, your prayer is not answered because you ask from wrong motives, trying to satisfy your lusts. ⁴Unfaithful creatures! Don't you know that to make friends with the world is to become God's enemy? ⁵Or do you suppose that scripture has no meaning when it says, "God yearns jealously over the spirit which God has put within us"? ⁶Yet God's grace is stronger. Scripture also says: "God withstands the arrogant but gives grace to the humble." ⁷Surrender then to God. Resist the devil and the devil will run from you. ⁸Draw near to God and God will draw near to you. Sinners, cleanse your hands. You who are double-minded, purify your motives. ⁹Be sorrowful, mourn and weep. Let your laughter be turned into mourning and your joy into gloom. ¹⁰Humble yourselves before God and God will raise you high.

Throughout his letter James offers an antidote to the jealousy, rivalry, the "spirit within us that yearns toward envy" (4:5; literal translation). That antidote is humility, another name for simplicity, for wisdom. The root meaning of humility is *humus*, soil. A humble person is one who receives everything from God, who accepts "soil," creaturehood as the basic reality of human existence. Receiving from God is the way to humility, patience, meekness, wisdom, every good gift (1:5, 6, 7, 12, 17, 21; 4:2-3; 5:7, 10). Listening and learning, open to God and to others is a way to humility (1:19; 2:5; 5:11). Humility is not passivity, but receptivity. It is certainly not groveling before God or others; it is simply accepting truth, learning from every situation, growing in simplicity and in wisdom.

3:13-18

> [13]Who is wise and knowing among you? Let such a person show by good conduct how to work with the meekness that comes from wisdom. [14]If your hearts are full of bitter jealousy and rivalry however, do not exult, do not lie against the truth. [15]This is no wisdom from above but is earthly, sensual, demonic. [16]Wherever there is jealousy and rivalry, there is tumult and worthless activity. [17]Wisdom from above, however, is pure and full of peace. It is gentle, docile, full of mercy, fruitful. Such wisdom is without uncertainty and is straightforward. [18]The fruit of justice is sown in peace for those who practice peace.

As you read these verses, recall someone whom you consider wise. You may be able to list even more aspects of wisdom than James as you remember the wise one in your life.

In these verses James first depicts a worldly wisdom. Like some other NT authors, James sees "the world" as a source of evil (4:4). Instead of thinking of James' "world" as a physical place (so full of natural beauty), think of it as a domain of power, a dynamism which drags us away from God's sphere, God's reign.[5]

The wisdom which is a gift of God is then characterized (v. 17). There is today much discussion of psychologist Eric Erikson's life stages and how they relate to our spiritual growth. The final stage of human development for Erikson, hopefully to be achieved late in life, is integrity. Our own

[5]Brian McDermott, SJ, *What Are They Saying About the Grace of Christ?* New York: Paulist, 1984.

experience of the gift of wisdom is that it can operate at any time in life. Wisdom does correspond with Erikson's stage of "integrity," being whole, authentic. Unlike Erikson's stage, however, wisdom is not so much a goal of our lives nor a task as a gift, continually given in our lives.

Community

A second aspect of a biblical spirituality which differentiates it from other Christian spiritualities is that our response to God's initiative is communal. In the Jewish scriptures, God calls and saves a people. In the NT we are a new Israel, the Body of Christ, a new family called into existence by God's adopting love, bonded with one another in all the ways we relate to God by the Spirit. This communal spirituality does not negate our unique and individual relationship with God, but enhances it. When using scripture to nourish our spiritual life, it is always important to keep alert to the community dimension of spirituality. Thus, we focus now on James' specific injunctions about justice, sin and healing in the Christian community.

1:27-2:7

²⁷Religion which is pure and faultless before God our Father is this: to care for orphans and widows in their distress and to keep oneself untainted by the world.

2 My brothers and sisters, you have faith in our Lord of glory, Jesus Christ, not in respect to other people. ²Sometimes a person enters a synagogue, dressed in expensive clothes, laden with gold rings, and at the same time a poor person dressed shabbily comes in. ³You attend to the one who is richly dressed and say, "Sit in this place of honor," whereas to the poor person you say, "Stand over there or sit at my feet." ⁴Do you not thus make distinctions and judgments based on evil thinking?

⁵Listen, my very dear sisters and brothers. Hasn't God chosen the poor of this world to make rich in faith and heirs to the kingdom promised to all who love God? ⁶Here you have dishonored the poor. Is it not the rich who oppress you yourselves, dragging you to court and ⁷blaspheming the good name by which you are known?

"My beloved brothers." James inserts this warm and personal touch very often in his homily. "Brothers" seems to be a technical term for Christians, a kind of shorthand, and so a more appropriate translation would be "My beloved brothers and sisters." James calls God Father (1:17, 27; 3:9) and thus sees our responsibilities toward each other in community flowing from our new family of adoption. In 1:27 James echoes Israel's prophets (Is 1:1-10), but he adds the father/family relationship as the source of our true worship, which is care for the helpless.

The whole community in these times of persecution seems to be helpless, outcast, orphaned by Roman and Jewish society. The rich oppress, drag into court, blaspheme the name of Christ (2:6-7). So why this alignment with the rich and powerful, even within the community? James asks. Israel was commanded to welcome the foreigner because once it was a foreigner in Egypt. James exhorts us to welcome the poor person because we ourselves as a community are poor and powerless. Even the rich in our community are poor if they truly act as brother and sister because *we*, as community, are poor and powerless.

That may be difficult for first world Christians to believe. But all of us, whatever denomination, are brother and sister to the poor and powerless Catholic, Methodist, born-again

Christian in the third world. Our family is God's poor. Once we are baptized, this is our family. We cannot be separated from them by our geography, our pretenses at power, our posturings and prestige. We can close our hearts to them but they remain our blood. We can pretend to be different, separate from the Christian winos on skid row, the Christian guerrillas of El Salvador, the Christian garment workers of Korea, the Christian dictators of Latin America, but we are brothers and sisters.

Only blind and willful ignorance can keep us closed to the sights and cries of the poor. In baptism, however, we are gifted with wisdom. That means we are graced to be open and receptive to God's word. When we hear God's voice in the cries of the poor, how can we act on God's word? Let us listen again to James.

4:13-16

[13]Come now, you who say, "Today or tomorrow we will go into such and such a town and spend a year there and trade and get gain"; [14]whereas you do not know about tomorrow. What is your life? For you are a mist that appears for a little time and then vanishes. [15]Instead you ought to say, "If the Lord wills, we shall live and we shall do this or that." [16]As it is, you boast in your arrogance. All such boasting is evil. (RSV)

"Whoever knows what is good and does not do it commits sin," James concludes. Then he begins to denounce the rich within his own community:

5:1-5

5 Come now, you rich, weep and howl for the miseries that are coming upon you. [2]Your riches have rotted and your garments are moth-eaten. ³Your gold and silver have rusted, and their rust will be evidence against you and will eat your flesh like fire. You have laid up treasure for the last days. ⁴Behold, the wages of the laborers who mowed your fields, which you kept back by fraud, cry out; and the cries of the harvesters have reached the ears of the Lord of hosts. ⁵You have lived on the earth in luxury and in pleasure; you have fattened your hearts in a day of slaughter. (RSV)

"You have both condemned and murdered the righteous, yet they do not resist you," James concludes. The plans of the powerful perish, the boasts of the arrogant wither, the wealth of the rich turns against them. "Weep and howl." The unpaid wages of the cheated poor cry out and the Lord hears. James is not writing to wicked pagans. He is writing to the Christian community. The scriptural Word is addressed today to our first world Christian churches, to our own "fattened hearts" (5:5). What is the remedy? How can we offer true worship which is care for the helpless? How can we become more deeply identified with our powerless brothers and sisters? James exhorts us to "be patient" (5:7). We have fattened our hearts with luxury and pleasure, but James writes, "be patient."

5:7-12

⁷Be patient, brothers and sisters, until the Lord comes. Look how the farmer waits patiently for the precious fruit of the earth while it receives the early and the late rains. ⁸So you be patient. Make your hearts firm because the Lord's coming draws near. ⁹Do not murmur against one another, my sisters and brothers, lest you be judged, because the judge is standing at the door.

¹⁰As an example of patient suffering, my brothers and sisters, take the prophets who spoke in God's name. ¹¹We count those who endure as blessed. You have heard of Job and his endurance, and how in the end, the Lord was very compassionate and full of mercy. ¹²Above all, my dear sisters and brothers, do not swear, either by heaven or by earth or by any other oath. Let your yes mean yes and your no mean no, lest you be judged.

Perhaps there is no direct connection between this passage and the excoriation of the rich which precedes it. Scholars say James' maxims are not necessarily logically arranged. I propose an interpretation then, which is based on the gospel parable of the wheat and the weeds. The master in that parable says, let them grow together and at harvest we will separate the wheat from the weeds. James, in this passage, tells us to "build up our hearts" in preparation for the Lord's coming, the harvest (vv. 7-8). Who can say whether his or her spiritual life is choked with weeds or healthy with wheat? To measure and soul-search, to scrape and scruple is not to receive from God. To be patient, to wait humbly on the Lord for growth, is what James seems to advise us rich, luxury-laden, even murderous (5:6) Christians. Let the wheat and weeds of our lives grow together and let the Lord's judgment, not our own, decide our fate. "Be patient until the coming of the Lord."

We need patience with ourselves as we take baby steps toward social justice. We need the Spirit to open our eyes, ears, hearts. We need to receive justice and care for the poor as God's gifts to us. To be materially poor and powerless is not an ideal in itself. We need God to wean us gradually from abusing power and pleasure so that we can feel in solidarity with our third world family. We need God to wean us from our sense of entitlement so that we can use our political power to offer a counter-cultural witness to our first world family.[6]

James next offers two examples of how God weans: the prophets and Job. The prophets, some of whom were prestigious priests or aristocrats, spoke out for justice, even in the courts of kings...and were persecuted. Job was immensely wealthy... and learned wisdom when he was stripped of his power and riches. What is the end, purpose, goal of God in this? The Lord is multi-compassioned and full of mercy (v. 11). God has a variety of ways to communicate compassion to us. When we have received that compassion, basked in it, absorbed it, God's own compassion can flow through us. Because God is full of mercy, God calls us, rich and poor as we are, to share the divine purpose as best we can, to mediate mercy as best we can to the helpless, the outcast, the hungry of the world.

5:13-20

[13]Is anyone among you in trouble? Let the person pray. Is anyone cheerful? Let that person sing praise. [14]Is anyone among you sick? Call for the elders of the congregation to pray over the person, anointing the sick with oil in the name of the Lord. [15]A prayer with faith will save the sick person. The Lord will raise

---

[6]Gustavo Gutierrez, *A Theology of Liberation*, Maryknoll, N.Y.: Orbis, 1973. Denis Edwards writes of three possibilities of finding God as we slowly align ourselves with the powerless: 1) We can experience sorrow and guilt, for God is gracing us in that guilt; 2) We can work directly with even *one* who is poor, handicapped, underprivileged so that we can receive from that one, for God is the real giver; 3) We can taste our helplessness, our dependency when our attempts to effect justice are frustrated, for God is sure to nourish. (Denis Edwards, *The Human Experience of God*), New York: Paulist 1983, pp 77-84.

up the sick, forgiving past sins. [16]Therefore, confess your sins to one another and pray for one another, in order that you be healed. The prayer of a good person has great power and is effective. [17]Elijah was just a human being, weak like ourselves. He prayed fervently that it might not rain and for three and a half years it did not rain. [18]Then he prayed again, it rained, and the land brought forth crops.

[19]Brothers and sisters, if any one of you strays from the truth and another of you brings that person back, [20]know that whoever leads a sinner back from wandering ways will be saved from death and will have a multitude of sins cancelled.

As you read this passage, ask yourself, when do you pray? In times of pain, in times of joy, James exhorts us to pray. When we are sick the leaders of the community pray and anoint and the Lord saves/heals, raising us up, forgiving our sin.

Confessing our sins to one another is another source of healing in the community. At this time in the church there was no rite of reconciliation. Baptism was the only sacramental source of forgiveness. Sin was not confessed to the leaders of the community, but "to one another." Perhaps pagans commented "See how they love one another" because Christians were not parading their virtue before one another but confessing their sinfulness. So often we are disarmed and led to love by another's admission of guilt, failure, weakness, sin. Confession often begets confession; we know we are not alone in the struggle for truth, justice and love. In the final verses of his work, James asks us to speak the truth to one another in love.

James does not give us a program for Christian community.[7] He does highlight our prophetic solidarity with the weak,

[7]Dietrich Bonhoeffer, *Life Together*, New York: Harper & Row, 1954.

sick and sinful, and our prophetic call to confront the rich and powerful. Our baptism has constituted each of us prophet to the community and to society. A prophet is one steeped in the Word of God, who hears God's Word of comfort to the oppressed, who hears God's Word of challenge to the oppressors and who dares to speak it and act on it. If we hear and do not act . . . .

Just a tiny step for justice, taken at God's invitation, can have wonderful effects. Even if such a first step has no visible results, God is at work. We are not alone. The whole community, the church, is hearing a renewed call to be prophetic: to be immersed again in scripture, and to find there the impetus and the courage to criticize more stringently the structures of society and to console more effectively the victims of injustice.

Faith Flowing Into Action

James has emphasized how receptive the Christian is to be to God's gifts of wisdom, healing, saving. Biblical spirituality recognizes that it is God who initiates the relationship. God communicates, reveals, lavishes on us life and love, invites us to respond to grace, to mystery. James knows that, and reminds us that a major response to God's initiating love must be faith which flows into action.

For almost nineteen centuries commentators on James' homily have wrestled with the relationship between faith and works,[8] contrasting James' understanding with Paul's asser-

---

[8]Kugelman, pp. 27-35, offers a brief and clear statement of this relationship, drawing on ancient and contemporary interpreters of *James*.

tion in Romans 3:28 (also see Rom 4:2-5) that faith alone justifies us, sets us right with God, saves us. Martin Luther's commentary on *James* which dismisses "works" and opts for Paul's "justification by faith alone," fueled reaction from the Roman Catholic hierarchy some 400 years ago. The debate still sometimes continues in the way Protestants and Catholics relate with God. For example, accepting Jesus as personal savior is sometimes contrasted with earning merit or with observing the Ten Commandments.

What does James himself teach on the relationship between faith and works?

2:14-26

¹⁴What good is it, my brothers and sisters, if someone claims to have faith, but has no works. Can faith save such a person? ¹⁵If a brother or sister has nothing to wear and lacks daily meals ¹⁶and you say: Go in peace, be warmed, be filled — and you do not care for their bodily needs, what good is that? ¹⁷Thus faith, if it is not expressed through works, is dead.

¹⁸Someone will say however: You have faith and I have works. Show me your faith without works and I will show you my faith expressed through works. ¹⁹You believe that there is one God. Right. Even the demons believe that and tremble. ²⁰Are you willing to learn, foolish one, how faith without works is fruitless? ²¹Wasn't our ancestor Abraham made righteous by works when he offered his son Isaac on the altar? ²²You see that faith and works operated together in him and by works his faith was completed. ²³Scripture was fulfilled thus: Abraham believed God and it was counted as righteousness; he was called the friend of God. ²⁴So you see that a person is made righteous by works and not only by faith. ²⁵In the same way, Rahab the prostitute was made righteous by works. She entertained the enemy messengers and sent them away by a different route.

²⁶Just as the body without spirit is dead, so faith without works is dead.

Read this crucial section slowly, preferably out loud. What is your own understanding of the relationship between faith and works? Before Abraham was ready to sacrifice his son, before the child was even conceived, God initiated a relationship with Abram and promised him descendants. In response, "Abram put his faith in Yahweh who counted this as making him justified" (Gen 15:6). Faith from the time of Abraham until the later writings of the NT meant a surrender to God, a trust, a commitment, a response to God's initiating love. Works of love, care, service, justice, forgiveness, hospitality towards the neighbor; works of trust, obedience, single-heartedness, worship of God were meant to flow from Israel's relationship with God, the faithful One. The Ten Commandments, the 613 laws of Sinai, even laws regulating diet and religious observance were only further elaborations of the Israelites' basic response to God's covenanting love: faith. Faith, that response of Israel to God's faith, meant also a love returned, a commitment, an attachment to God who, ever so trustworthy, calls, chooses, saves, loves.

In the NT, Jesus criticized the Pharisees' reliance on Law as a means of earning God's favor. Paul emphasized faith as surrender to God in trust; this experience of salvation flows over into love. "In Christ Jesus. . . faith is working through love" (Gal 5:6). Even in later NT writings like *Ephesians* (2:4-9) and *Titus* (3:4-7), Christian teachers repeated a fundamental principle of biblical spirituality: God alone gifts us with salvation. In no way can we achieve, earn, merit grace or salvation.

Some first century teachers or their hearers must have erred, however. Perhaps they understood faith as adherence to truths about God and Jesus. Intellectual orthodoxy is, of course, no guarantee of relationship with God; even the demons can produce intellectual assent to truth, James writes (2:19). For James, with his Jewish spirituality, faith is relational, a response to God's initiating love. To be in relationship with God is to take God's concerns to heart. God does not need to command the royal law of love of neighbor (2:8). Because of our attachment to God, love becomes "like breathing out and breathing in." Any "faith" which does not express itself in this connaturality with God, in loving with the very heart of God, in doing the very works of God, especially love and justice, is dead (2:17).

What does James' teaching on faith mean for today's Christian? Our faith life tends yet to be centered on intellectual consent to correct doctrine; our moral life centered on law; our spiritual life on regular attendance at worship and regular personal prayer. A biblical spirituality, one which James and his community experienced, and to which James invites us, is much more relational. Faith, morality and spirituality are just different names for our responding to God's extravagant compassion for us, ways of being with God, in the very heart and mind of God and thus expressing God's mind and heart in the world.

God, James tells us from his own experience, is multi-compassioned (5:11). This word is James' own, never used in the LXX nor elsewhere in the NT. It captures, in the Greek prefix *poly* (many or multi) before the word for compassion, some of the extravagance and abundance of God's initiating love. Because we are united with a multi-compassioned God, compassion is meant to flow in a variety of ways from our community. Faith, morality and spirituality flow into action on behalf of others.

Summary

You have read and reflected on James' homily, putting your experience in dialogue with his. Perhaps, you would like to use *James* for prayer now. You might return to a passage that moved you to respond to God or Jesus with words, feelings, memories. Responding to God with any or all of our self, in word or in action, in awe or gratitude, praise or sorrow, anger or upset, joy or love, is prayer. Here are some leading questions for praying with *James.* Your responses might be shared with another or in a group.

● Remember as concretely as possible a time when God took the initiative in your life, surprised you with joy (1:17). Then share your feelings about that experience with God.

● What in you, your history, your life today blocks you from receiving all that God wants to lavish on you? Ask God to show you the blocks. Pray not to deny but to hear "the word of truth" which God wants to speak to you (1:18). Ask God to remove those blocks, to let life and love flow between you.

● Sit quietly, asking God how wishing well for the poor might be changed into some small action (2:15-16). Don't think and plan; wait for God to show you. Then respond with words and feelings. Be honest. If "some small action" overwhelms you, tell God just how you feel. Return often to this prayer until you are really ready to take that one small step. Then respond to God with action.

These three examples may give you an idea how to let God address the Word to you, how to respond with words, affections, memories, images, decisions, even distaste. Sometimes we feel dry, imageless, emotionless. Teresa of Avila teaches that prayer is a conversation with Someone whom we know loves us. In times of dryness then, we can simply read and/or listen to God speak through James' homily; our listening is an essential part of this conversation.

If you have read, reflected, perhaps even prayed with this homily you now have an experience of the spirituality of James and his community. How has their understanding of and relationship with God affirmed your own? How has their spirituality challenged yours and that of your family, community, church? How has the Spirit transformed you because of your interaction with God's Word?

I PETER

I PETER

● An early Christian reflection on baptism is at the heart of this letter. How do you understand baptism? When you were a child, how did you think of baptism? Has that meaning changed? What experiences have changed your understanding? What feelings and verbal response to God rise in you as you reflect on your baptism?

● One meaning of baptism is that it plunges us (*baptizō* means immerse in Greek) into the death and resurrection of Jesus. How does the death of Jesus influence your daily living? If you quickly shrug, "It doesn't" — wait. Be quiet. Ask Jesus to show you how you share in his dying day by day. Do the same for the resurrection. If the Spirit doesn't seem to be teaching you consciously, ask for the gift of sharing more deeply and with more awareness in Christ's dying/rising life. Try to pay attention to that movement during the week.

● So much of this letter is meant to offer us hope, not only for ourselves as Christian community, but for the world. Share with the Lord your hopes, dreams, desires; then show him and ask him to show you pockets of despair in your life.

Tell him your hopes and fears for your family, world, community. Listen to his response. Pray for the gift of hope.

● This letter advocates, as did Vatican II, a witness-to-the-world spirituality. How, in what specific ways, do you participate in secular society? List fifteen to twenty concrete participations: for example, reading a newspaper, voting, seeing a movie, playing on a sports team, etc. How would your participation be different if Christ were not important to you? Show your list to the Lord and consecrate each activity to him.

Introduction

This letter will resonate with post-Vatican II Catholics as we claim our responsibilities in and to the world. Like *James, I Peter* is addressed to Christians in "the diaspora," specifically the northern provinces of Asia Minor (now Turkey): Pontus, Galatia, Cappadocia, Asia and Bithynia. It is supposedly from Peter, the apostle, although the author also designates himself "fellow-elder" (leader), witness of the sufferings of Christ, and sharer in future glory (5:1). Since the letter concludes with references to Silvanus (perhaps Paul's co-worker, called Silas in Aramaic), Mark, and a Roman woman, it may ha e been the work of disciples of Peter who stood in his tradition but who would have written this letter of encouragement after Peter's death c. 64 A.D.* Most scholars do date it later, perhaps the 80's, and locate its origin in Rome.

While the letter has often been analyzed as a baptismal

*Indeed, the reference to the woman (5:13) may indicate the Roman community of disciples.

homily, even a liturgical program for a Roman baptism, scholars today are more willing to agree that it is indeed a letter, all of one piece. Its language is a polished Greek; its theology is often similar to Paul's; its spirituality is deeply permeated by biblical meditation, particularly on the Psalms and Isaiah 53; its methodology is that early Christian pattern of proclaiming good news and only then exhorting behavior in response to God's initiating love.

In focusing on God's initiative, the spirituality of *I Peter* is like that of *James*. There are other similarities in thought as well so that some think that this author may have had a copy of *James* before him. Certainly both authors advocate responsibility for justice in secular society and love within the community. However, Peter seems to address his letter to a lower economic class of Christians who are aliens, the politically, legally, socially dispossessed. These resident aliens may have included artisans and merchants, but tenant farmers and slaves in the rural areas of Asia Minor were major recipients of the letter.[1]

Their marginality was compounded by their baptism. Because emperor worship, idolatry "functioned as the ideological foundation of the empire," Christians were alien.[2] They were open to ridicule, economic boycott, and other ostracizing sanctions of their neighbors. Peter writes to encourage the "strangers" to find their home within the household of God, the Christian community. Experiencing such solidarity with

[1]John Elliott, *A Home for the Homeless*, Philadelphia: Fortress, 1981, pp. 148-149.

[2]Gerhard Krodel. "The First Letter of Peter," *Hebrews, James, 1 and 2 Peter, Jude, Revelation*. Proclamation Commentaries, Philadelphia: Fortress, 1977, p. 76.

one another, they will then find the courage to participate in every secular institution with inner freedom.

The spiritual life to which our author will urge them — and us — is one characterized by a contemplation of the dying and rising of Jesus which is "the decisive pattern of all Christian existence, indeed of all human existence."[3] Thus Jesus is central to the spirituality of this letter. In his sufferings and glory we can discover the meaning of our baptism and the basis for our hope; in his mission we can discover our own mission to society; in his person we can discover our leader in our pilgrimage to God.

Contemplation: A Consciousness and a Conscience

To lead a spiritual life, we need to be aware of the Spirit. Thus contemplation as awareness is often seen as the heart of any spirituality. In a biblical spirituality it is important to recognize God's initiating, extravagant, faithful love, to recognize God's call to and action within the Chrisitan community, to recognize God's mission for us as our faith flows into action. It is the gift and the task of contemplation which opens us — our eyes, our minds and our hearts — to that recognition of God/Spirit.

Much of this letter is an exultant reflection on baptism and its meaning. According to Donald Senior, this author makes a unique contribution to the New Testament and thus to Christian spirituality by noting how a new consciousness of God is an effect of baptism. "Baptism is 'an appeal to God for a

[3]Donald Senior, CP, *1 and 2 Peter*, New Testament Message, Wilmington, DE: Michael Glazier, Inc., p. 6.

clear conscience.' "[4] "Conscience" here (3:21) is the same Greek word as consciousness, used in 2:19 and translated as being "mindful of God."

Certainly one of the aspects of any spirituality is an expanded awareness which is usually called contemplation. Biblical contemplation differs from the usual meaning, however. For example, in his *Will and Spirit*, Gerald May writes of a contemplative spirituality in which consciousness is without content. May, who as a psychiatrist knows much about the mind and consciousness, lists some of the usual content of consciousness: thoughts, emotions, images, memories, hopes.[5] In many Eastern and Western spiritualities, a consciousness which transcends these "contents" is termed contemplative. In biblical spirituality, however, it is just those thoughts, emotions, images, memories and hopes which are the human response to God's initiating love. To contemplate, in a biblical spirituality, is to go outside our self, yet to use our whole person to respond. To contemplate is to pay attention to God, to be focused on Jesus, to listen to the Spirit.

Because of God's passion for self-revelation and self-communication, we have the creative, saving Word of Jewish scripture and the very embodiment of God's ultimate Word in Jesus. It is through the Word and through Jesus in a biblical, incarnational spirituality that God introduces us to the mystery of life and love and invites our response in dialogue. A Judeo-Christian consciousness then is shaped by the Word and surrenders to the Word, sometimes wordlessly but with words and images, emotions and actions as well.

[4]*Ibid*, p. 72.

[5]Gerald May, *Will and Spirit*, San Francisco: Harper & Row, 1982.

The actions are of course that Christian behavior which Peter advocates as flowing from conscience or our mindfulness of God. We are to "arm ourselves with the same thought" (4:1), literally "the same mind" as Christ.

In May's exposition of a contemplative spirituality, the consciousness is to be as serene as a still bowl of water, undisturbed by the turbulence of passion. Much of our own training in spirituality taught us to try to quiet our minds by quieting our desires and passions before prayer. Peter would concur if that stillness means the stripping away of self-illusion so as to be clothed with humility (5:5). It is consciousness of God which gives us a new vision of reality and that fear which means awe, wonder and reverence (1:17; 2:17; 3:2; 3:15) before the mystery of God which grounds all reality. Humility which Peter (like James) urges us to is simply the truth of who we are, before God and with each other.

Yet biblical spirituality is a passionate, not passionless, spirituality. Stoic philosophers, contemporary with the first Christians' mission to the Gentile world, were teaching that God was without passion, that God's greatest attribute was *a-patheia*, being without passion. Jewish leaders, prophets, and poets had always portrayed their Lord Yahweh as a God of deep passion, meaning both long-lasting emotion and far-reaching desire. The biblical spirituality of the early Christians gave way to Stoic influence. Spirituality is characterized today in many people's minds, as denial of emotion and ridding of desire. Biblical spirituality offers another possibility.

4:1-6

4 Because Christ suffered in his flesh, you must have the same mind as he has. Whoever has suffered in the flesh is finished with sin. ²Such people no longer live according to human desires but according to God's desire. ³ . . . Once you lived in licentiousness, lusts, debaucheries, carousing and lawless idolatry. ⁴The pagans cannot understand that you are now no longer running with them to every excess, and so they verbally abuse you. ⁵They will have to give an account to the one who is ready to judge the living and the dead. ⁶Why was the gospel preached even to these who are dead? In order that they might be judged in the flesh according to human judgment, but might live, in the spirit with the very life of God.

Peter tells us to arm ourselves with the mind of Christ who suffered (4:1). The Greek word for suffering is the same as passion, and indeed, we speak of the passion of Christ. To have a consciousness in tune with Christ's, however, can mean not only suffering with him, but feeling passionately with him, and desiring passionately with him.

"Christ suffered in the flesh" (4:1). There is another kind of "fleshly passion" or, literally, lust which Peter spells out in this same section: licentiousness, drunkenness, revels, carousing and lawless idolatry (4:3). These are lusts (often translated "passions") which are self-destructive tendencies (4:2-3; 2:11). But to share passion — suffering, emotion and desire — with Christ is to offer him compassion, com-passion. To compassionate Christ is to be out of oneself and deeply into him, his mind and his heart, and so to contemplate the Word made flesh.

Sharing in the Dying and Rising

The Word made flesh is portrayed by Peter as shepherd and servant, lamb and leader, even an *episcopos*, bishop (2:25, usually translated "guardian"). The overarching image of Jesus, however, is the suffering and exalted Christ with whom we are joined in baptism. Jesus in his activity of dying and rising is the center of all biblical spirituality for the Christian.

1:18-22

> [18]You know that you were ransomed from the futile ways handed on to you from your ancestors, redeemed not with corruptible silver or gold [19]but with precious blood, the blood of Christ, like an unblemished lamb. [20]Having been known from the foundation of the world, he was manifested in these last days for our sakes. [21]Through him you have a faith in God as the one who raised Jesus from the dead, the one who glorified him. Thus, your faith and your hope are fixed on God. [22]Purified by your obedience to truth which leads to sincere familial affection, love one another with all your hearts.

The word "ransom" (v. 18) has often troubled those Christians who tend to see God as a divine ogre, exacting the last drop of blood from this loveable man to appease God's wrath. Some medieval theologians who formulated doctrines of atonement and satisfaction imagined that Jesus' blood and torture[6] were necessary to placate a God who was infinitely offended by our sin. On the other hand, Thomas Aquinas taught that any action, no matter how insignificant, by the Word-made-flesh would have saved us. When St. Paul writes about ransom, he never says that Jesus pays any debt we owe

[6]Very early in church history, Marcion taught that the God of the Jews was an entirely separate (and hateful) deity from the loving Father of Jesus. He was condemned as a heretic. We continue Marcion's error if we hold that the God of the Jewish scriptures is vengeful and "just" whereas the God of the NT is loving and merciful.

to God. Peter, however, does teach that we are ransomed from our futile ways, from hopelessness. It is our own self-defeating behaviors from which we need to be freed, not from God's punishment.

In the opening lines of this letter we see the author's devotion to the blood of Jesus (1:2) as a sign of the new covenant which God has made with us in Christ. The symbol of blood so often used in the Jewish scriptures was not a sign of torture and pain but of sharing life, a covenant sign (Ex 24:3-8). Blood signifies a bonding of lives: God's with ours through the blood of Christ. Like the offering of the Israelites, a lamb's precious blood united us with God (1:19) and that Lamb of God is Christ. As in 1:2, so here in 1:22 our response to God's new covenant is invited: "obedience to the truth and sincere love of the brothers and sisters...from the heart." Our faithful hearing of the Word (obedience) is not required in itself but is always invited in response to such abundant love.

Notice that for the early Christians, the dying of Jesus could not be separated from his exaltation through the resurrection (1:20). Our hope is in God who glorified him.

2:4-8

⁴Come to our living stone, Christ, rejected by human beings, yet precious, chosen by God. ⁵You too are living stones, being fashioned into a spiritual house, a holy priesthood, to offer spiritual sacrifices acceptable to God through Jesus Christ. ⁶It stands written:

"Behold I lay a chosen stone in Sion, a
precious foundation stone. The one who
believes in it (him) will never be ashamed."

> 7For you who believe, he is honored, but to unbelievers, the stone which was rejected by the builders has become the cornerstone. 8This stone, for unbelievers, has come to be a stumbling block, a rock of scandal. They stumble because they disobey the word.

Have you ever experienced God as a rock, an image so often used in the Psalms? Here Jesus is imaged as a stone, a large foundation stone. The slaughtered Lamb of God and the Suffering Servant are images of Jesus in his dying/rising. The stone rejected and later established as cornerstone is another image which Peter reflects on as he tries to articulate the centrality of this mystery of Christ. The rejected one is raised. Jesus is a living stone. He is alive!

2:18-25

> 18Servants, submit yourselves respectfully to those who govern you, not only to the good and considerate, but also to evil rules. 19This is grace: if, because of consciousness of God, anyone bears grief, suffering unjustly. 20What good is it if, sinning, you suffer a beating. If while doing well you endure suffering, this is a grace in the eyes of God. 21To this you were called. Because Christ suffered on your behalf, he leaves behind an example so that you may follow his way. 22He certainly did not sin, nor did he ever speak deceitfully. 23When reviled, he did not revile in return. When suffering, he did not threaten, but delivered himself to the one who judges justly. 24He carried our sins in his body, carried them up to the tree so that we, dying to sin, might live for justice. By his bruising you have been healed. 25Once wandering like sheep, you now have turned to your shepherd and supervisor (*episcopon*, overseer, bishop).

Read Isaiah 53 and then compare this description of Jesus' sufferings, his attitude toward this violence, and the long-term

effects of his passion. Early Christians were puzzled. How
could a man who spent his whole life doing good (Acts 10:38),
such an innocent man, have suffered so viciously, so vio-
lently? As they reflected on their own lives, joined to Jesus' by
baptism, they became increasingly aware that their lives now
were full of suffering on account of him. Our author is aware
of the kind of mental and emotional persecution these Christians of Asia Minor face. He offers them the example of Jesus'
breaking the cycle of evil and violence by absorbing it in his
body, his psyche, refusing to pass on insult and hatred. By his
wounds, our own "needs" to do acts of violence, revenge, and
hatred — while undoubtedly remaining a temptation in every
aware human person — are healed.

This passage as you have discovered is based on one of
Isaiah's Servant songs — usually termed the Suffering Servant
Song. Isaiah himself saw a community, the Israelites, as the
Servant. Through Israel's suffering exile in Babylon, other
nations would see God's light and be saved. Then God would
rescue, heal, and vindicate the Servant Israel (Is 53:10-12).
Various applications of the Suffering Servant were made to
historical figures through the centuries. For example, the
Essene community of Qumran at the Dead Sea applied these
words to their victimized founder, the Teacher of Righteousness (c. 180 B.C.E.).

When the Twelve and other apostles began to preach the
resurrection of Jesus to their compatriots, the Jews scoffed.
They knew that anyone who hung upon a tree (that is, upon a
wooden cross) was cursed by God. Jesus, according to Deuter-
onomy 21:23, was cursed. How could the disciples convince
Jews of God's vindication of Jesus? They would use the very
authority of the Jews themselves, the scriptures. In pondering

the words of Isaiah 53, the apostles could see that the original application of this Servant song to Israel could be just as well applied to the sufferings of Jesus. They could show their contemporaries that Jesus' innocent suffering had redemptive value for all the nations. It was all part of God's plan, revealed through the prophet Isaiah. The Servant, once the community Israel, was seen to be Jesus himself. Perhaps Peter implies that now the young church of Asia Minor has become a Suffering Servant in a communal sense (5:9-10). Today the suffering-servant-church of the third world still witnesses God's desire for redemption of even the oppressors.

Not only is Jesus held up as an example for those who suffer, Jesus empowers us to die to sin and live to justice (sometimes translated righteousness or even holiness). Not only is he to be fixed before our eyes as example, Jesus is to live and motivate our hearts when we face injustice. It is *his* sufferings which we share.

4:12-16

> [12]Beloved, do not be surprised at the fiery ordeal which comes upon you to prove you, as though something strange were happening to you. [13]But rejoice in so far as you share Christ's sufferings, that you may also rejoice and be glad when his glory is revealed. [14]If you are reproached for the name of Christ, you are blessed, because the spirit of glory and of God rests upon you. [15]But let none of you suffer as a murderer, or a thief, or a wrongdoer, or a mischiefmaker; [16]yet if one suffers as a Christian, let him not be ashamed, but under that name let him glorify God. (RSV)

What causes suffering in your life? Reflect and jot down your ideas. Although this passage refers to our suffering as

Christians, we first-world Christians have little opportunity to be reproached for the name of Christ. We may be able to remember an incident or two when we suffered discrimination because of our alignment with Christ. However, we are all called to share his sufferings. How?

We all suffer, sometimes on account of our own willfulness, but often because we have lost some good, have been blamed unjustly, cannot effect a reconciliation — all those sufferings you jotted down above. Did Jesus ever suffer anything similar? The first Christians did not first search their Jewish scriptures to see how they should live, to find norms of behavior. First, they lived life wholeheartedly. Then they reflected on their experience, to see where and how the Spirit was working in and through their lived experience. They held up the incidents of their family life, work relationships, community life, ministry and mission to their scriptures and eventually to the dying/rising and life of Jesus.[7] They expected to find the pattern of Jesus' dying and rising in their own sorrows and joys. So Peter has only to remind them: look at your alienation in light of Jesus' pain — you could have expected it.

You are blessed (4:14). To bless means to hand over one's whole self. When Jesus shares his sufferings, he is pouring out all that he is into the life of the one whom he blesses. But his life is not only dying. It is his risen life shared which is the source of our joy.

1:6-9

> [6]In this you rejoice, though now for a little while you may have to suffer various trials, [7]so that the genuineness of your

[7]Luke Johnson, *Decision Making in the Church*, Philadelphia: Fortress, 1983.

faith, more precious than gold which though perishable is tested by fire, may rebound to praise and glory and honor at the revelation of Jesus Christ. [8]Without having seen him you love him; though you do not now see him you believe in him and rejoice with unutterable and exalted joy. [9]As the outcome of your faith you obtain the salvation of your souls. (RSV)

Joy is the major tone of this letter, joy in the midst of suffering. When have you experienced joy after or during or because of suffering?

In these few verses in which joy is exultant, Peter discusses faith. When we admire someone who is suffering, we often comment on the person's strong faith. A passage like this encourages the equation of faith with steadfast, courageous perseverance in the face of adversity. It is true that God's faith means God's fidelity, and our faith is a response to his fidelity to us. But lest faith come to mean Stoic constancy, Peter reminds us that we love Jesus.

In loving Jesus we believe in him (adhere to him, are committed to him) and "rejoice with unutterable and exalted joy" (v. 8). Again, it is our sharing Jesus' dying and rising, that is, loving him, which leads to joy. Our joy is a sign of salvation (4:13).

Baptism

Participation in the dying and rising of Jesus is a chief effect of baptism. Although many of us have been taught that baptism is a washing away of original sin, Peter expands that understanding. In 1:22, his reference to our having purified our souls probably indicates baptism.[8] Peter offers much more, however, for our reflection.

Baptism is a celebration of God's mercy and our salvation, a call to a new identity, a life-long empowerment.

3:18-22

> [18]For Christ also died for sins once for all, the righteous for the unrighteous, that he might bring us to God, being put to death in the flesh but made alive in the spirit; [19]in which he went and preached to the spirits in prison, [20]who formerly did not obey, when God's patience waited in the days of Noah, during the building of the ark, in which a few, that is, eight persons, were saved through water. [21]Baptism, which corresponds to this, now saves you, not as a removal of dirt from the body but as an appeal to God for a clear conscience, through the resurrection of Jesus Christ, [22]who has gone into heaven and is at the right hand of God, with angels, authorities, and powers subject to him. (RSV)

This is a classic passage on baptism. With allusions to Noah, the waters of destruction seem much more apparent than the waters of salvation. This passage shows us Peter's own biblical spirituality, how his own experience of baptism leads him to reflect on and celebrate God's mercy in rescuing Noah and his family. It also indicates Peter's global awareness. As he realized how the world-wide Christian community was sharing in the sufferings of Christ (5:9-10), here he focuses on the resurrection of Christ as the subduing of all cosmic powers, the resurrection as the source of our salvation. Our

[8]Senior, p. 25.

faith, that is our participation in the dying/rising Christ, saves
(1:9).

2:9-10

> ⁹But you are a chosen race, a royal priesthood, a holy nation,
> God's own people, that you may declare the wonderful deeds of
> him who called you out of darkness into his marvelous light.
> ¹⁰Once you were no people but now you are God's people; once
> you had not received mercy but now you have received mercy.
> (RSV)

Peter celebrates God's initating, saving love. He has
reflected on the prophet Hosea who, in response to God, had
at first named his children "Not my people" and "Unloved"
(Hos 1:6-8). In God's plan for Israel's and our salvation,
however, "Not-my-people" and "Unloved" will be re-born in
baptism and re-named by God: "God's people" and "Loved-
by-the-Lord" (Hos 2:1). We are born anew through the living,
abiding Word of God (1:23). We are called. Being called by
God and being loved constitutes the baptized one with a new
consciousness (3:21; 4:1) and a new identity.

Our new identity is described in 2:9.

> You are a chosen race,
> a royal priesthood,
> a holy nation,
> God's own people,
> empowered to tell the good news. . .

To a group of resident aliens what good news it is to know a
new home, to become a new race, a new nation, God's own
possession. Baptism has introduced them into the household
of God. As they have been invited to share in the life, death

and glory of Jesus, they have been invited to share in a new community. That community according to the Fourth Gospel was created by the dying/rising of Jesus "who died to gather into one family all the scattered children of God" (Jn 11:52). In baptism we are initated into that family which is chosen, royal, priestly and holy.

Our catechetical instruction today teaches us that in baptism we become prophet, priest, and royal-born. Most Catholics only have a dim remembrance of that teaching. If prophets predict the future, if priests say Mass and hear confessions, if kings and queens are mere figureheads, no wonder our new baptismal identity seems so meaningless, so vague. With a biblical spirituality, however, we can uncover new energies flowing from our new identity.

Prophets in scripture were those who were so attuned to God's mind and heart that they could speak for God. Instead of making specific predictions involving a one-on-one correspondence, prophets could promise God's fidelity and kindness to those who were oppressed. They could criticize the oppressors, chiding, challenging them with the Word of God. For us to claim our prophetic identity, we must make fruitful the union into which we have been plunged (*baptizō*). Thus united with Christ and having put on the mind of God/Christ (4:1) we can see life with God's/Christ's vision, can speak God's/Christ's word of consolation or challenge within our communities and/or to society.

Our experience of priesthood is male leadership in sacramental celebrations. For us to claim our baptismal priesthood, we must turn to the more biblical understanding of the priestly people. When the Temple in Jerusalem was destroyed (587 B.C.E.), when the people lost their place of sacrifice and public worship, they began to realize what later the Fourth Gospel articulates: God is not worshipped on certain mountains or in certain rites but "in spirit and truth" (Jn 4:23-24). Worship in spirit and truth surely encompasses our Christian sacraments, but reaches far beyond the seven, which were only defined and enumerated in the Middle Ages.

In Peter's time, there were no Christian priests, and while bishops may have presided at certain worship services, in the far-flung rural areas of Asia Minor the priestly prayer of a priestly community was probably the public and communal worship that approximated our Eucharist today. There was at that time no sacramental rite of reconciliation; instead each Christian confessed his or her sin and sinfulness to another and the community forgave in the name of Christ. Because there were no established church buildings for worship (the Christians of Peter's time assembled in homes), worship was an attitude that probably permeated the whole day of the priestly people.

Christians had a sense of the glorified, risen Lord that seems sharper than our own. Perhaps, with so many of them slaves or former slaves, or at least subject to despotic emperors or self-serving governors, the Lordship of Jesus was a felt and joyful experience. To share in his risen life through baptism must have filled them with an appreciation of their own dignity as participants in his Lordship. Their new birth in baptism made them royal born, a kingly people. They became heirs to all that Jesus won in his dying and rising: a whole, free, joy-filled creation, a kingdom of justice and peace, of truth and love.

Peter also calls them and us a holy nation. Baptism invites us to holiness as God is holy (1:15-16). All our morality will flow not from our will power and virtue, but from God's holiness. Joined to Christ in baptism, we not only continue Jesus' prophetic, priestly and royal mission to the world but become channels of God's/Christ's holiness. We are living stones being built and shaped into a new, living, holy house of God, based on our cornerstone, Christ (2:5).

This house of God image in no way implies that we are a static entity, a church building as it were. We are empowered (a better translation of 2:9) to tell the good news. No wonder "the church is mission" has been a post-Vatican II theme applied to all of us, not just foreign missionaries. Another effect of baptism is this good news: God has called us "out of darkness into God's marvelous light," — an image of moving into hope.

Baptism empowers us for mission, the evangelization which Vatican II assures us is the task of the church who is each of us and us as community. Our being empowered, our claiming our baptismal identity, is a life-long process, a "growing up to salvation" (2:2-3). As we die and rise daily in union with the death and resurrection of Jesus, as we celebrate God's mercy and our salvation, as we reflect on and gradually appropriate our new baptismal identity, we continue to be empowered as signs of hope and joy to an increasingly despairing and desperate first world society.

Signs of Hope

1:3-5

> [3]Blessed be the God and Father of our Lord Jesus Christ! By his great mercy we have been born anew to a living hope

through the resurrection of Jesus Christ from the dead, [4]and to an inheritance which is imperishable, undefiled, and unfading, kept in heaven for you, [5]who by God's power are guarded through faith for a salvation ready to be revealed in the last time. (RSV)

"We have been born anew to hope . . ." What are some signs of hope in your personal life? family or commuity life? in the nation? the world?

"Born-again" Christians are making a dynamic impact on society. Catholics too are born again in baptism and more and more of us are beginning to claim the power and energy (*dynamis*) that flows from the resurrection and our baptism into it. This energy and hope is not pie-in-the-sky, fluffy optimism but a power within us which springs from and leads back to suffering, as Peter so well understands. The dying and rising dynamic Jesus introduced within us at baptism will continue to our death.

William Lynch, S.J., has studied some of the most pain-filled human beings of our society, the mentally ill. In *Images of Hope* he writes how this sickness springs from apathy, which he describes as "all will and no imagination." The mentally ill lack energy because they have no desire, no *eros*, just will. Lynch criticizes some of our past training in spiritual discipline:

> People are sufficiently fearful of energy and life without making it worse, without elevating the fear to the level of a principle and a virtue.[9]

[9]William Lynch, SJ, *Images of Hope*, Notre Dame, IN: University of Notre Dame, 1974, p. 139.

Energy and life in abundance are signs of hope and health (wholeness, salvation, healing, *shalom*, peace). So are trust and dependency.[10] Hope is a relationship, Father Lynch explains throughout his book, in which God shows us again and again how we can depend on God, waiting, longing to receive. Hope is an attitude toward life, an attitude which sets us free.

Opening to the gift of hope given us in baptism, we grow ever more mentally free, free from the need to absolutize, to achieve intellectual certainty, free to imagine alternatives, to create. We gradually grow more emotionally free, free from false dependency, fear, apathy, and denial of our humanity, our limits, even our denial of death.[11] We grow more spiritually free, as we "set our hope more fully on the grace that is coming..." (1:13), and relax our need to earn favor, gain merit, win God's approval, achieve our salvation.

Hope is neither passivity nor optimism. Hope in Christ's tomorrow is not happy optimism. Because it is born from Jesus' sufferings and our baptismal share in them, our hope is

> ...realistic enough to look human evil, illusion, and even death straight on. It acknowledges our inescapable limits.[12]

Nor are we just to sit by, passively waiting for the end of the world. In Jesus' resurrection the end of the world has begun. His resurrection has consecrated, christened human life; has harnessed, christened human energy. According to Jürgen

---

[10]John L. McKenzie, "Salvation," *Dictionary of the Bible*, 15th Edition, New York: Macmillan, 1979, pp. 760-763.

[11]Ernest Becker, *The Denial of Death*, New York: The Free Press, 1973.

[12]David Myers, *The Inflated Self*, Minneapolis: Winston-Seabury, 1980, p. 149.

Moltmann, baptism for the early church "symbolized the beginning of the new creation of the world in the rebirth of a human being."[13] Baptismal hope is "hope in action."

Hope in Action

When I Peter was written, Christians were demoralized by their alien status in society. Thus the author reminds them of their new and communal identity as God's own household, royal-born, priestly, holy people. Even if they were in society as "slaves, women and others of low social rank,"[14] their cohesion within God's household, the Christian community, strengthened them to witness to the very institutions which ostracized them. Donald Senior calls theirs a "witness spirituality."[15] The word witness in Greek is *martyr*. Even though there was no widespread bloodshed during those decades of early church life* by their witness Christians were "martyred," sharing in the sufferings of the innocent Jesus.

Physical dying for Christ has sometimes been termed red martyrdom. Women and men religious giving up wealth, sex, and power experienced white martyrdom. Irish missionaries who left the Emerald Isle were said to have suffered green martyrdom. The fact is, baptism does constitute us all as martyrs, witnesses to the dying/rising and life-giving Christ.

[13]Jürgen Moltmann, *Hope for the Church*, Nashville: Abingdon, 1979, p. 49.

[14]Elliott, p. 149.

[15]Senior, p. 14.

*except for Nero's persecution of the Roman community.

Our hope energized into the action of witness provides a home for the homeless, calls us to godly behavior, breaks the cycle of violence, and urges us to participate in every human institution.

4:7-11

> ⁷The end of all things is at hand; therefore keep sane and sober for your prayers. ⁸Above all hold unfailing your love for one another, since love covers a multitude of sins. ⁹Practice hospitality ungrudgingly to one another. ¹⁰As each has received a gift, employ it for one another, as good stewards of God's varied grace: ¹¹whoever speaks, as one who utters oracles of God; whoever renders service, as one who renders it by the strength which God supplies; in order that in everything God may be glorified through Jesus Christ. To him belong glory and dominion for ever and ever. Amen. (RSV)

Paul has lists of those gifts which build up community. Here is Peter's list: prayer, love, hospitality, speaking and ministering (literally, serving). Whom do you know in your Christian community having one or more of these gifts?

One of the first witnesses we offer the world is that "the Christian community constitutes a home for the alienated and estranged." [16] This witness of welcoming the marginalized and outcast is becoming more evident not only in third world countries but also in our own first world emphasis on social justice. These gifts are given to build the cohesion of the community where the alienated can find hospitality — or so we hope.

[16]Elliott, p. 223.

2:11-12

> ¹¹Beloved, I beseech you as aliens and exiles to abstain from the passions of the flesh that wage war against your soul. ¹²Maintain good conduct among the Gentiles, so that in case they speak against you as wrongdoers, they may see your good deeds and glorify God on the day of visitation. (RSV)

By maintaining good conduct among the pagans, we witness to them, Peter explains. Two missionary principles used by the rabbis seemed to have influenced the first Christians' missionary tactics: identify with those you want to evangelize ("To the Jews I become as a Jew . . . to the weak I become weak, that I might win the weak" I Cor 9:20-22); and be submissive to those whom you want to win over ("I have made myself a slave to all that I might win the more" I Cor 9:19). Because the early church had such a sense of urgent mission, a compelling need to invite pagans to hear the good news, Christian slaves thus were exhorted to be obedient, Christian wives submissive. All were to "win" pagan hearts with their reverent behavior (2:13-14, 18; 3:1).

Slavery was not the issue then as it has become in the last few centuries because Christians believed that the world was about to end (2:18). Wives' "submission" to their husbands is urged so that husbands "may be won" to obedience to the word (3:1), a missionary technique. If the husbands are Christian they are exhorted to good conduct too. "Husbands, live considerately with your wives" (3:7). The word for "considerately" is literally "according to knowledge." This exhortation is not to kindness then but to raised consciousness. The new knowledge is of the equality of men and women. They are "co-heirs of the grace of life." This new consciousness, which baptism has effected, assures our dignity, unity and equality as men and women in Christ.

3:15-17

> [15]but in your hearts reverence Christ as Lord. Always be prepared to make a defense to any one who calls you to account for the hope that is in you, yet do it with gentleness and reverence; [16]and keep your conscience clear, so that, when you are abused, those who revile your good behavior in Christ may be put to shame. [17]For it is better to suffer for doing right, if that should be God's will, than for doing wrong. (RSV)

Our last passage ended with the hope that the pagans would glorify God for the Christians' good deeds. Good conduct, however, often provokes jealousy. Peter notes that we may have to give an account of the hope that is in us, and suffer unjustly (2:19). We can witness to society by our gentleness, reverence, and submissiveness in the face of this unjust hostility. Like Jesus' meekness before insult and even torture (2:21-24), we can break the cycle of evil by blessing instead of reviling and revenging ourselves. "Do not return evil for evil...but on the contrary, bless" (3:9).

2:13

> [13]Be subject for the Lord's sake to every human institution, whether it be to the emperor as supreme...

"Be subject for the Lord's sake to every human institution..." Peter continues, listing those "institutions": emperors, governors, slave-masters whether gentle or overbearing, and husbands. Peter's letter is unique in the New Testament because it achieves a balance between viewing human governing institutions as servants of God (*Romans*) or as demonic (*Book of Revelation*).[17]

The central focus of this letter is how baptismal hope might be lived in active participation in human creation. "Creation" is the literal meaning for "institution." To be subject to does not mean conform to; to be subject means to participate in.[18]

We see in *I Peter* the seeds of what we know today: that secular society is also sacred society by reason of the resurrection and our leavening influence.

> The Christian is not to withdraw from the institutions of human society, even when they present conflicts with one's beliefs. Instead one must "submit," participate "for the Lord's sake," because in leading an authentic Christian life in the midst of the world one can further the creative task of God himself [sic] as he [sic] moves the world to its destiny.[19]

Sometimes to witness to hope, to lead an authentic Christian life will mean discerning and then perhaps risking a counter-cultural witness: standing over against some institutions today, criticizing some human creations, protesting unjust governmental policies. That witness to authenticity will undoubtedly involve bloodless martyrdom as our hope becomes active in today's society.

Our Leader

We began our reflection on Peter's letter with the central figure of Jesus before us. We conclude with one last contem-

[17]*Ibid*, pp. 73-92.

[18]Senior, p. 43.

[19]*Ibid*, p. 7.

plation of Jesus, our leader on pilgrimage to God. Because Peter addresses resident aliens, people who do not belong, we find an undercurrent in his letter that encourages us all toward our goal (*telos*) who is God. Peter uses movement images, pilgrim images.

While we heed John Elliott's caution not to spiritualize the plight of a really marginalized people of the first century,[20] I believe that the text of *I Peter* can question and challenge us who seem so comfortably ensconced in our middle class security. We can believe that "the Christian community constitutes a home for the alienated and estranged."[21] If we are to get in touch with our own alienation, we, in English-speaking countries at least will have to concentrate on our symbolic destitution and estrangement, our yearning for more, for deeper relationship with each other and with God. In this spiritual uprootedness, we turn to Jesus as leader.

To Christians who have been brought out of darkness, hopelessness, ransomed from the ways of futility (1:18), Peter directs us toward the goal, the "*telos* of your faith: salvation" (1:9). He urges us to gird up the loins of our minds (1:13) using the imagery of the Passover, the beginning of the exodus when Israelites were to eat their meal in readiness to move, standing, "with loins girt." Christians are to be moving to the goal, God, with mental alertness, with awareness and sense of direction. Indeed our faith and hope are "towards" God (1:21). Peter invites us to "come to him," to Jesus (2:4), words which evoke tenderness and trust; to follow Jesus' steps (2:21). Jesus is always in the process of setting our direction, of

[20]Elliott, p. 17.

[21]*Ibid.*, p. 233.

bringing us to God (3:18), an experience which we will study further in *Hebrews*. As our shepherd and leader, Jesus himself has "experienced the redemptive process . . . he walks with us in the struggle to reach God." [22]

Summary

As you have read sections of Peter's letter, as you have reflected on and responded to the good news, you have been putting your own lived experience in dialogue with that of "Peter" and his community. You have not only a better understanding of their baptismal commitment but hopefully you have begun to develop the gifts given you in baptism: a contemplative consciousness, a sharing in the dying and rising of Christ, a joyful hope and action within and on behalf of the world. Now I invite you to deepen your appreciation of *I Peter* by praying with it.

Read the entire letter slowly, stopping to respond when a word, phrase, idea, image touches you. Respond in silence or with words, with feelings or with memories, with song or with dance. Response to the Word is prayer. Hopefully, this process will take several days, perhaps weeks.

• How has your love of God, of Jesus and of others changed because of your encounter with "Peter" and his community? How has the Spirit been transforming you in your study and prayer? What more do you want from the Spirit? Be specific, be bold, be passionate in your desires, your hope!

[22]Senior, p. 70.

● What will your witness to the world look like — today, in the near future, when you are elderly? Ask the risen Lord to show you his desires, his hope for you. Sit quietly to see what "bubbles up." Don't censor these thoughts and images. After you have finished this prayer period, jot down any ideas which you remember. Don't rack your brain; if the Lord wants you to remember, he'll bring it to mind.

● Read your list during your next prayer period. Note what feelings arise in you when you pay attention to what "the Lord" desires for your witness to the world. I put "the Lord" in quotes because if feelings of guilt or compulsiveness or disturbance accompany "the Lord's" desires for you, these desires may not be from him. Respond to his desires with desires of your own as well as some small step of witnessing today.

HEBREWS

HEBREWS

● *Hebrews* has been called a theology of hope. Whom do you know who is hopeful? Did you grow up in a hopeful family? If so or if not, what were the causes of hope or hopelessness? Remember a time when you felt hopeless. How did you ever emerge from those feelings?

● This author interprets the Jewish scriptures in the light of Jesus' saving work. What parts of the Old Testament nourish you? Remember what you can of those parts in some detail. Why are they meaningful?

● What was a moment of liturgical worship that really caught you up? Do these liturgical highpoints occur often? If so, can you pinpoint some causes? If not, what can you do to make liturgy more meaningful?

● *Hebrews* presents Jesus as very, very human. What are some of his very human qualities that you admire? Try to remember specific gospel stories and be concrete in naming your favorite qualities. Open to a gospel at random and see whether the evangelist is focusing on Jesus' humanity. How does Jesus' being human make you feel?

● *Hebrews* explains that the Word of God is like a two edged sword, probing us deeply. We have been making the Word of God our home as we read, study and pray with these "catholic epistles." If we do that, we are promised, we will know the truth and the truth will set us free (Jn 8:32). Where do you want the Word to open up truth and freedom in you? Where do you still want to hide from the Word's probing?

● To prepare to enter the mind and heart of our author, carefully and prayerfully read Jeremiah's description of the new covenant which *Hebrews* celebrates: Jer 31:31-34. Then pray Psalm 40. Imagine the boy Jesus praying this psalm with his parents. Imagine him studying it as a young man. Imagine him praying it in prison as he awaited his trial. How does he feel? How do you feel?

Introduction

Hebrews is a homily. Its author calls it a "word of exhortation" (13:22) and there is emphasis not only on the author's word, but on the Word of God. The author is not Paul, as even the early church leaders knew, citing differences in style, language and key concepts such as the meaning of faith. Speculation in the third century and in our own has suggested Paul's co-workers: Priscilla, Barnabas, or Apollos as author. Our unknown author understood Judaism well, and was well trained in the Greek translation of the Jewish scriptures, the Septuagint (LXX). His or her Greek is probably the best in the New Testament. There is some debate about the author's immersion in Greek thought, specifically the philosopher Plato's categories of shadows and copies. Roman Catholic scholars tend to see a neoplatonic influence in *Hebrews*.

Although addressed to "the Hebrews," we cannot tell from

the text what city, even what nationality received this exhortation. We do know the addressees had never seen Jesus. They knew their LXX well. The "Hebrews" were discouraged and tempted to apostasy, that is a denial of their faith, their commitment to Christ. They hankered after their old religion.

This author tries various approaches to urge them forward. His or her major focus is Jesus, exalted, interceding for his people, the great hero and pioneer of faith who was tempted just as "the Hebrews" are being tempted now. Jesus is the source of our hope, the powerful Word of God to whom all scripture points, our compassionate high priest through whose sacrifice we have been saved from sin, from fear of death, from the futility (7:18) of the old law and cult. Yet, the author never denigrates the worship of Israel, but simply points out that for all its richness, it didn't work. Jesus has offered us something "better," a word used thirteen times.

To elucidate the spirituality of our author, I invite you to read portions of this homily before reading my comments. First I will treat that "better hope" (7:18-19) which we have through Jesus, a hope based on God's promises made apparent in God's Word of scripture. Then I will keep "our eyes fixed on Jesus" (12:2), his humanity and his work on our behalf, particularly his sacrifice. Finally I will investigate two responses we twentieth century Christians might make to such a leader and priest: liturgical worship and a life of discerning obedience.

Hope Based on God's Word

6:17-20

> [17]God, wishing to show more surely to the heirs of the promise God's own unchangeable will, intervened with an oath.

> [18] . . . Now because it is impossible for God to lie, we, taking refuge, have strong encouragement for taking hold of the hope that lies before us. [19]This hope is an anchor of the soul, firm and reliable; this hope enters into the inner shrine [20]where our forerunner, Jesus, entered on our behalf. . . .

These three verses summarize much of the homily. God's promise and God's oath are unchanging and true. Because of God's fidelity, we have "a strong consolation." Hope is set before us for our grasping. Paul used the image of reaching out to take hold of Christ who had already taken hold of him (Phil 3:12). Our hope could be Christ himself whom we grasp, Christ an anchor for our "psyche." Instead this author says that Jesus has run before us to enter, on our behalf, "inside the veil," that is, the heavenly sanctuary. There is a pilgrim theme throughout the homily, a movement toward the future which always, for the Christian, indicates hope for the future. At first we are urged to hold fast, then to advance (6:1) and finally, to run (12:1) to the throne of God. What our author has contributed to the notion of pilgrimage is that Jesus not just accompanies us, not just goes before us, but *runs* ahead to blaze he way into the future, leading us with great eagerness very close to God.

10:19-25

> [19]Therefore, friends, we have the confidence to enter the sanctuary by the blood of Jesus, an approach [20]which he inaugurated for us through the veil, a new and living way (that is, of his flesh). [21]Having a great priest over the household of God, [22]let us approach with a true heart in full assurance of faith. Our hearts are sprinkled, cleansed from an evil conscience, our bodies washed with pure water. [23]Let us hold fast, confessing our hope

without wavering, for the one who promised is faithful. [24]Let us be considerate of one another for the purpose of stirring up love and good works, [25]not abandoning the assembly as some do, but encouraging each other so much the more as we see the day drawing near.

Hope is a gift given in community and for community. Hope is to be a public witness, and a community en-courage-ment. Because Jesus has dedicated his blood (a literal translation of v. 20) and his flesh for us, we approach with confidence (v. 19). In a full assurance of faith, our hearts are made true, which in Jewish thought means faithful, especially in relationships. Faithful hearts are the results, not of our own virtue, but of the fidelity of the One who makes the promises. God's fidelity is the cause of our fidelity, our faith, our hope, and the source of our community's love, good works, and assemblies.

3:6 — 4:11

[6]Christ, as son, is in charge of God's household. We ourselves are God's household if we cling to that boldness and boasting which accompany hope.

[7]Therefore, as the Holy Spirit speaks:

Today if you hear God's voice, [8]do not harden your hearts as in the rebellion, just as the day of temptation in the wilderness [9]where your ancestors put me to the test. They saw my works for forty years. [10]Therefore I was angry with this race and I said, "Always they go astray in matters of the heart. But these, they do not know my ways." [11]So I swore in my anger, they shall not enter into my rest.

[12]Be alert, friends, lest an evil heart of unfaithfulness lead any one of you to fall away from the living God. [13]Rather, encourage one another every day so long as it is called "today" so that no one of you be hardened in deceitfulness of sin. [14]We have

become sharers in Christ, if indeed we hold fast to our first confidence, steadfast until the end. [15]It was said:

Today if you hear God's voice, do not harden
your hearts as in the rebellion —

[16]Did not some of the ones who heard rebel? Were they not the ones leaving Egypt, led by Moses? [17]Or with whom was God angry for 40 years? Not with those who sinned, whose corpses fell in the desert? [18]Or to whom did God swear not to enter into rest if not against those who disbelieved? [19]We see that they were not able to enter on account of infidelity.

4 Therefore, a promise of entering God's rest remains. Let us fear lest any one of you think to fall short. [2]We too have received good news just as they did, but the word was of no benefit to those who were not united by means of faith with those who heard. [3]For we, the ones who believed, go into the rest just as God said:

"As I swore in my anger, they will not enter into my rest," although the works had come into being from the foundation of the world. [4]For it said somewhere concerning the seventh day:

"And God rested on the seventh day from all works." [5]And again in this,

"They will not enter into my rest."

[6]Therefore it remains that some enter into it, but those who received the good news formerly did not enter on account of unfaithfulness. [7]Again, God appoints a day "today," saying through David, later as it was spoken before:

"Today if you hear God's voice, do not harden your hearts." [8]For if Joshua had caused the people to rest, God would not have spoken later of another day. [9]A sabbath rest, then, does remain for the people of God. [10]Whoever enters God's rest rests from works, just as God rested. [11]Let *us* hasten, then, to enter into that rest so that no one may fall in this pattern of unfaithfulness.

God's fidelity is constantly hymned throughout scripture. I selected for you to read this long and somewhat obscure interpretation of the Israelites' wandering in the desert just to offer an example of how deeply our author is steeped in scripture, its divine promises and human hope.[1] Every argument this author puts forward to convince his/her wavering community to hope is scripturally grounded. This is not a preacher's exercise in logic. It is an expression of a biblical spirituality, a relying on God's word revealed in scripture.

God's word is a "word of power" (1:3), a word of salvation (2:1-3). Salvation is in the spoken word, the revelation of God's own self. Yet our author, who believes so firmly in scripture's power and authority, uses a wonderful freedom in quoting, changing words, merely alluding that "someone testified somewhere" (2:6-9). No chapter and verse bludgeoning of his/her hearers. This kind of biblical spirituality calls for meditation, prayer, integration of the whole message of scripture in its context. The author of *Hebrews* uses thirty-six direct quotations from the Jewish scriptures and, in a very integrated way, makes at least eight clear allusions to them.[2]

God's word is not a lesson in ancient literature. The word is being spoken for us TODAY, the author exclaims, through the Holy Spirit (3:7, 13). The author shows us how the early church theologized from the scriptures in practical, behavior-oriented ways. Christians can find all the models for practical

[1]Reginald Fuller, "Hebrews," *Hebrews, James, 1 and 2 Peter, Jude, Revelation*, Proclamation Commentaries, Philadelphia: Fortress, 1977, p. 10. The whole of *Hebrews* is a midrash, an interpretation of Psalm 110.

[2]Juliana Casey, IHM, *Hebrews*, New Testament Message, Wilmington, DE: Michael Glazier, Inc., 1980, pp. 19-20.

action we need in this sacred word. For example, in 13:2, Christians should offer hospitality because when Abraham did, he discovered that he was entertaining angels.

Chapter 11

The author inundates us with models of faith. Although you may not be familiar with the situations spelled out in this chapter or with all these men and women mentioned, at least read the list of Jewish heroes and heroines of faith quickly. If you would like the background for these stories read *Hebrews* by Julianna Casey, pages 75 to 80. You might want to add some of your own favorite models of faith, Christian saints of years ago, Christian saints who surround you today in family and community, parish and country and world.

11:39-40

[39]And all these, though well attested by their faith, did not receive what was promised, [40]since God had foreseen something better for us, that apart from us they should not be made perfect. (RSV)

In this homily, faith is described not as an attitude within us but an objective reality which is God's promise, God's fidelity. God is the guarantee. God is our faithfulness. Our hope flows from God's unchanging promise. Faith keeps our eyes fixed on God, as these men and women have demonstrated with their lives and deaths. These are the "cloud of witnesses," and yet they did not receive that "something better" which God had in store for us.

12:1-2

> **12** Therefore, since we are surrounded by so great a cloud of witnesses, let us also lay aside every weight, and sin which clings so closely, and let us run with perseverance the race that is set before us, [2]looking to Jesus the pioneer and perfecter of our faith, who for the joy that was set before him endured the cross, despising the shame, and is seated at the right hand of the throne of God. (RSV)

The something better is someone better. Jesus is himself our better hope.

> The law perfected nothing. On the other hand, a better hope is introduced through which we draw near to God (7:19). (RSV)

The fidelity of the whole community of Israel (ch 11) has found a better expression in Jesus' fidelity. Our hope, our faith, our fidelity, our perfection depend on Jesus, the pioneer and perfecter of our faith. Faith means a fixing of our eyes, a seeing beyond apparent realities to the reality of Jesus exalted, Jesus who endured our very temptations to lose hope and courage, who faced shame and fear and death. He sets the pattern for our faith, he is the reason for our hope. This is *Hebrew's* major theme in exhorting its discourged, wavering hearers or readers. What Jesus has begun, he will complete, make perfect, bring to the goal (the literal meaning of "perfect"). Jesus himself shows that faith means endurance.

10:32-36

> [32]But recall the former days when, after you were enlightened, you endured a hard struggle with sufferings, [33]sometimes being publicly exposed to abuse and affliction, and sometimes

being partners with those so treated. ³⁴For you had compassion
on the prisoners, and you joyfully accepted the plundering of
your property, since you knew that you yourselves had a better
possession and an abiding one. ³⁵Therefore do not throw away
your confidence, which has a great reward. ³⁶For you have need
of endurance, so that you may do the will of God and receive
what is promised. (RSV)

Hope gives confidence (10:19, 4:16) and endurance. Hope
leads us to "do the will of God." And there's the rub. The will
of God has been so maligned through the ages that good, holy
people whom I know fear getting too close to God because
they say "Look what God did to Jesus" when Jesus prayed,
"Thy will be done," in his agony in Gethsemane. Even Teresa
of Avila scolded God for testing her with too many hardships:
"No wonder you have so few friends." Of coure, the worst
misuses of the term "will of God" are those supposed-to-be-
comforting remarks to victims of tragedy. "It must be God's
will."

What is God's will? Another way to phrase the question:
What does God want for our world, for our community, our
family, ourselves? What does God passionately desire? Sometimes just changing the noun "will" to the verbs "want" and
"desire" opens up new understandings. As we turn now to fix
our eyes on Jesus (12:2), we will discover that *Hebrews* has a
devotion to God's will for Jesus akin to Jesus' own devotion in
the Fourth Gospel: "My meat and drink is to do the will of
God who sent me" (Jn 4:34).

Jesus

1:1-4

1 After God had spoken in times past in many and various
ways to our ancestors through the prophets, ²in these days God

spoke to us in a son appointed heir of all, through whom God also made the worlds. ³This son is a reflection of God's glory and a stamp of God's substance. Bearing all things by means of his word of power, the son made, in himself, purification from sins. Then he sat down at the right of the Majesty in the heights. ⁴He has become so much better than the angels and has inherited a name more excellent than theirs.

At regular intervals throughout this homily, our author will focus our attention on Jesus. All our morality and spirituality flow from our attraction to him who loves us so dearly . Since Jesus is the very center of all truly Christian spirituality, and the measure of our spirituality, it is appropriate that we read these passages with care and with prayer.

The verses above are a prologue, somewhat like the Fourth Gospel prologue's "In the beginning was the Word..." The Word of God in the Jewish scriptures tried to alert the Israelites, tried to communicate God's abundant love to them. The people, however, could not seem to understand the message which God tried to get through to them in "many and various ways" in the Jewish scriptures. Finally God embodied the Word in the flesh of God's own son so that we "in these last days" would just have to get the message.

Hebrews, John's Gospel and, earlier, the Wisdom literature of the Old Testament associated the Word and the Wisdom of God, personified as Lady Wisdom who helped God create the world (Wis 8:1; Prov 8:30; Wis 7:22, 26). The Word, like Lady Wisdom, is the radiance and the image of God, we are assured (Heb 1:3). From now on in *Hebrews*, however, the Word/Son/Jesus will be characterized not by his being, who he is, but by his function, what he does — and what he does is always on our behalf.

Jesus has made purification for sin. In many and various ways our author will spell out how and when and why that is Jesus' major mission. As a result of his mission, God exalted him and gave him the name above all names, even the angels'.

Jesus' name is Son. When the theme of "today" recurs later in this homily, the "today" is the day of Jesus' exaltation, his sitting in glory with God. Instead of fastening on his bodily resurrection as the triumph of Jesus, *Hebrews* attends to his exaltation as the final victory over sin and death.

2:9 — 3:6

[9]We do see Jesus, the one who for a little while was made less than the angels, Jesus, who on account of the suffering of death, was crowned with glory and honor so that he, by the grace of God, might taste death for everybody.

[10]When Jesus began to lead many children to glory, it was fitting for God, for whose sake all things are and through whom all things are, to make the leader of their salvation perfect through suffering. [11]For the one making holy and the ones being made holy, all are one. For this reason Jesus was not ashamed to call them brothers and sisters, [12]saying:

I will announce your name to my brothers and sisters; in the midst of the assembly I will sing praise to you.

[13]And again,

I myself will place my trust in God.

And again,

Behold, I myself and the children whom God has given me.

[14]Since, therefore, children have shared blood and flesh, Jesus also shared with them in the same way so that he might destroy through the death the one who has the power of death, (that is, the devil) [15]and might free those who, through fear of death

through all of life, were subject to slavery. ¹⁶Surely Jesus does
not take hold of angels, but he does take hold of the children of
Abraham. ¹⁷Jesus had to be made like his brothers and sisters in
everything. In this way he might become a merciful and faithful
high priest before God, in this way he expiates the sins of the
people. ¹⁸By virtue of that fact, he himself has suffered, having
been tempted so as to help those being tempted.

3 So then, brothers and sisters, holy ones, sharers of a heavenly
calling, consider the apostle and high priest of our confession:
²Jesus, who is faithful to the one who appointed him, just as
Moses was in the whole of his household. ³For this one, Jesus,
deserved greater glory than Moses since the one who builds the
house has greater glory than the house. ⁴Now every house is
fashioned by somebody, but the one who fashioned everything
is God. ⁵Moses was faithful in his whole household in the
capacity of "servant," bearing witness to the things which were
going to be spoken. ⁶Christ, as son, is in charge of God's
household.

How do you relate to Jesus? What do you call him?
Hebrews calls him an apostle. What does an apostle mean to
you? He is also called in this section a pioneer, brother,
deliverer, priest, householder. Do any of these ways in which
Jesus acts on our behalf appeal to you? Why or why not?

Our author, using scripture, wants to show that Jesus is
superior to the angels and to the great heroes of Israel: Moses,
the founder of the house of Israel, and Joshua, their leader into
the Promised Land. Jesus is especially superior to the levitical
priests, for he is a merciful and faithful high priest.

It seems very bold of our author to assert that being human
is what gives Jesus the edge over the angels (2:5). Three times,
the author will marshal scripture quotes to show how human
and brotherly Jesus is, in solidarity with us, sharing flesh and

blood with us. "The Christology of Hebrews is primarily about relationships."[3]

This particular passage seems to gain a new timeliness in this age of nuclear fear. Jesus acts as deliverer for all those who through fear of death were all their lives slaves of that fear. Ernest Becker won a Pulitzer Prize in 1976 for *The Denial of Death* which exposes modern society's fears, denials, attempts to waylay, even conquer death. Jesus has tasted death on behalf of everyone. God has exalted Jesus, our pioneer through death to life. If we know in our heart, our whole being, not only in our believing minds, that Jesus is alive, is Lord, then we can be sure of our own final victory over suffering and death. Jesus has carved the way through pain, defeat and death to life.

Do we know of his life and his Lordship in our whole being? If we have not "tasted" that experience, we may-must certainly beg God to know the exalted Lord. If we do know him that intimately we, like him, still need to trust God's power over death. Jesus, tempted to lose trust and hope and courage in the last days of his earthly life, perhaps prayed the psalm which the author of *Hebrews* attributes to him: "I will put my trust in God."

Notice that God made Jesus perfect through suffering. Perfection is a word used nine times in this homily, three times applied to Jesus. But our author makes it a passive verb. God makes Jesus perfect (5:9 and 7:28 as well); Jesus makes us perfect. It is not our activity on behalf of ourselves, our salvation, our holiness. Perfection here has none of its modern connotations: keeping the law of God, conforming to the

[3]*Ibid*, p. 48.

customs of family or society, practicing virtue, making no mistakes. The word comes from the Greek word for goal, or completion. God brings Jesus to the goal: exaltation. Jesus leads us toward the goal: God. To be aimed toward our goal is "perfection." Jesus (v. 11) makes us holy, brings us to completion, to fulfillment. It is not our task.

Jesus makes us holy, pioneers our salvation, frees us from fear of death and from the devil who once was the master of death, and helps us who are tempted. Most fundamentally, however, for this author, Jesus makes propitiation for sin (2:17). Another way to phrase it is expiation, the wiping away of sin. In Hebrew, the word is *kippur* (Yom Kippur, Day of Atonement). *Kippur* is always God's action. God wipes away our sin. We will have more to say on this central event of our salvation below.

The next few verses, 3:7-4:11, we have already studied in the context of the biblical foundations of our author's spiritual integration and rational argument. In this section of our study of Jesus, apostle, one who is sent on mission, we might re-read those verses in terms of Jesus' leadership. His liberating action is like a new exodus for we Christians who follow our pioneer towards God's "rest" which is still open to us as sharers in Christ (3:14).

4:14 — 5:10

[14]Having, therefore, a great high priest who has passed through the heavens, Jesus, the son of God, let us hold fast to our confession. [15]We do not have a high priest unable to show compassion, unable to share in the suffering connected with our weaknesses, but one who has been tempted in everything in quite the same way, apart from sin. [16]Let us come near,

therefore, with boldness to the throne of grace so that we might receive mercy and find grace as a help coming at just the right time.

5 Indeed, every Jewish high priest, chosen from human beings, is appointed on behalf of human beings with respect to things of God so that the priest might present gifts and sacrifices for sins. [2]He is capable of dealing gently with the ignorant and misled, since he too is surrounded by weakness. [3]So the high priest must make offerings for people, as well as for his own sins. [4]Now no one takes this position of honor for himself but is called by God as Aaron was. [5]So too the Christ did not glorify himself in becoming a high priest, but God said to him:

You are my son; I have begotten you today.

[6]Likewise God says in another place:

You are a priest for eternity according

to the order of Melchizedek —

[7]Jesus, in the days of his flesh, offered up prayers and supplications with loud cries and tears to the one who was able to save him from death. [8]Having been heard as a result of reverent fear, although he was a son, he learned obedience from what he suffered. [9]Having been made perfect, he became for all who obey him a cause of eternal salvation, [10]having been designated by God high priest "according to the order of Melchizedek."

In our first passage on Jesus, he was emblazoned before us in exalted glory, the very radiance of the Father. Then we were shown how faithfully, mercifully he who is in such solidarity with us as brother, leads us, always acting on our behalf. In this third passage Jesus' humanity is again emphasized but a new and quite central motif is expanded: Jesus is our high preist.

He is able to be so compassionate with us because he has shared every one of our temptations. Every one. The early church fathers would assert that unless Jesus experienced every bit of our humanity then our humanity is not completely saved: "What is not assumed is not saved." If we think only of his three temptations in the desert, with perhaps some hard moments during his agony in the garden, we may have a very foreshortened understanding of Jesus' life. The author of *Hebrews* uses a Greek verb which indicates that Jesus was tempted all through his life. That is consoling. None of us will probably "speak" with Satan or even have to elude those who would puff up our pride and "make us king" (Jn 6:15). It is the day to day weariness, the grumblings and grudges, the little hungers after honor, money, sex, status, security which tempt us as they tempted Jesus.

Jesus, however, was "apart from sin" (4:15). In the Hebrew worldview, there were two kinds of sin: missing the mark (note the goal-oriented language of archery) and sin "with a high hand" (Num 15:30). Jesus never sinned with a high hand, which means he never rebelled against God, never disobeyed God. Jesus freely reinterpreted the Law of God, the Torah. He disobeyed religious and cultural customs. To disobey God, however, means literally to refuse to hear God. Jesus never refused, although he was tempted to close God out from his life as he wrestled in the garden of Gethsemane.

Whenever we read and try to integrate scripture into our own lives, we must try to put on the mind of the author. Neither this author nor Jesus himself would understand today's Catholic terminology of mortal and venial sin. Perhaps Jesus did do a number of actions which those pre-Vatican II examination of conscience books might call venial sin. He was annoyed with his disciples' stupidity. He repudiated his mother for her lack of understanding (Mk 3:21 and 31). He undoubtedly whipped the innocent along with the guilty while chasing out money changers.(Jn 2:14-17). He cursed (Mk 11:12-14, 20) and insulted (Mk 7:27).

Other generations had other ways of classifying sin. St. Augustine would distinguish between sins of malice and sins of weakness. Jesus never evidenced malice, but he certainly showed weakness. He may well have missed the mark. In fact to be human is to be a misser of the mark, our target who is God. To be human is to be not-God. Luke's gospel tells us twice that Jesus not only grew in wisdom and age, which we would expect of a human person, but Jesus also grew in grace. Jesus grew more and more open and receptive to God's life within him.

It may be that we have often called sin what is simply human: annoyance, misunderstanding, harshness, discouragement, boasting, pleasure-seeking. One particular misconception of sin still afflicts many Catholics: we often equate temptation with sin. The error probably stems in great part from Jesus' saying: to lust after someone is already to have committed adultery (Mt 5:27-28); or from the Jewish commandments about coveting, wanting, as sin. If we read Jesus' statement in context, we see that the Lord was trying to help us internalize our morality. For a Christian it is not enough to keep outwardly the natural law against adultery. Our hearts are to be chaste, we are not to "use" another for our own pleasure even though no one else knows about it. The statement does not mean we are not to admire a beautiful person or want to be sexually united with a good person but that we are not to use another, even in our private thoughts. We may be tempted to use another. We can, if we are not afflicted with a compulsive personality disorder, choose not to use someone, even mentally.

Wants, thoughts, ambitions, even lusts, need not be denied, repressed, quickly buried. These movements of the human spirit are important to our own growing in wisdom and grace and help us to discover and discern what will please God. Jesus himself would be less than human if he did not experience these movements of the heart. These admirations and desires may have been temptation for him or they may have been joy.

Next, in our passage, we learn about the Jewish high priest, and how Christ, by reason of his exaltation, has made this Jewish institution obsolete. The Jewish high priest offered gifts and sacrifices for sins (5:1); Jesus offered his own prayers and petitions, offered loud cries and tears, offered himself. Jesus was afraid (5:7). This verse is *Hebrews'* version of the agony in the garden. We may image Jesus' agony like the famous picture in which he kneels, hands clasped on a rock, eyes serenely turned up where an angel offers a cup. *Hebrews* images the agony in a violent portrait but undoubtedly one more true to human experience. Jesus is begging, pleading, terrorized in the face of torture and death. The Greek word for "loud cries" means the screams of a wild animal which is trapped. Remember the noise of a zoo, an angry, fearful animal noise. Now imagine Jesus screaming at the top of his lungs: Father, save me!

This picture may offend modern sensibilities. It should. Some of us may have even been taught that Jesus was rapt in the beatific vision during his passion, while hanging on the cross. Not according to this author. There was no sweet serenity, no peaceful union with God. Mark's gospel claims that Jesus felt utterly abandoned by God and that in that desertion he cried loudly (Mk 15:34, 37). If we have sanitized the agony and the crucifixion, this author challenges us to see

Jesus tempted like us, frightened by death like us, collapsing, screaming in anticipated pain.

God was teaching him obedience through this terror. Obedience means to be able to hear God and to respond to what we hear. Jesus needed to learn how to respond in this "hitting rock-bottom." God taught and God made him perfect, brought him to fulfillment, made him the source of our own freedom in face of fear and pain and death.

7:25-28

> He remains forever. [25]Jesus is able to save for all time those who come to God through him, always living to intercede for them. [26]Indeed such a high priest was fitting for us. He is holy, innocent, undefiled, separated from sinners, having become more exalted than the heavens. [27]He did not have a need every day as did the high priests to offer sacrifices, first for his own sins and then for the people's. For this he did once for all, having offered up himself. [28]Yes, the law appoints those who are weak as high priests, but the word of the oath which comes after the law appoints a son, made perfect forever.

In this passage we learn that Jesus lives forever to make intercession on our behalf (also 9:24). If, as children, we learned the various kinds of prayer: adoration, thanksgiving, contrition and petition (or intercession, which technically is for others' needs rather than our own), we probably also learned that petition/intercession was the "lowest form" of prayer. Yet Jesus is not spending his risen life in adoration of God but in intercession for us.

In the Hebrew language the word for pray means "to ask." It comes from a root word which means "to stroke the face of God." As Jesus intercedes for us, we might imagine him using that intimate gesture. When you intercede for family and friends, for nations and peoples, remember that you are joining Jesus' own prayer, drawing near enough to stroke God's face with him.

10:5-14

> ⁵Consequently, when Christ came into the world, he said,
> "Sacrifices and offerings thou has not desired,
>   but a body hast thou prepared for me;
> ⁶in burnt offerings and sin offerings thou hast taken no
>   pleasure.
> ⁷Then I said, 'Lo, I have come to do thy will, O God,'
>   as it is written of me in the roll of the book."
> ⁸When he said above, "Thou hast neither desired nor taken pleasure in sacrifices and offerings and burnt offering and sin offerings" (these are offered according to the law), ⁹then he added, "Lo, I have come to do thy will." He abolishes the first in order to establish the second. ¹⁰And by that will we have been sanctified through the offering of the body of Jesus Christ once for all.
> ¹¹And every priest stands daily at his service, offering repeatedly the same sacrifices, which can never take away sins. ¹²But when Christ had offered for all time a single sacrifice for sins, he sat down at the right hand of God, ¹³then to wait until his enemies should be made a stool for his feet. ¹⁴For by a single offering he has perfected for all time those who are sanctified. (RSV)

Psalm 40 opens the selection above. It states that God does not want sacrifices and holocausts. What does God want? What is the will of God for Jesus? Take time to reflect on that question, to ask God to respond to you.

Our author understands that God wants the Word to take

a body, to become flesh, to be human like us in all things, except sin. Then, God wants Jesus in his human solidarity with us to be obedient, to pay attention to the voice of God in the various situations of living, loving, dying as a human being. God wants Jesus to offer his whole life, his body (10:10) which learned and loved, played and preached, hungered and hurt, comforted and critiqued, cried and clapped, raged and rejoiced. Any one action of Jesus would have saved us, teaches Thomas of Aquinas. How wonderful then that in his saving he experienced all that we experience from birth to death.

In 10:19-20 we learn that through Jesus' blood which he dedicated for us, and through his flesh, exalted now, we have a way to come close to God. This is not eucharistic symbolism, but an assurance that all that is of human flesh and blood is made holy, consecrated by Jesus' solidarity with us in our humanity. We are not to escape from our humanness, not to shun or despise our flesh. The gnostic heresy which afflicted the early church, the times of St. Augustine, and which recurred in Jansenism insisted that the human body is evil and the soul is supposed to break free from it as from a prison by works of "mortification." As first-born of embodied human beings, Jesus demonstrates the glory of flesh and blood made holy. It is in our bodies, through our bodies that he sanctifies us.

12:1-3

> **12** Therefore, since we are surrounded by so great a cloud of witnesses, let us also lay aside every weight, and sin which clings so closely, and let us run with perseverance the race that is set before us, ²looking to Jesus the pioneer and perfecter of our faith, who for the joy that was set before him endured the cross,

despising the same, and is seated at the right hand of God. ³Consider him who endured from sinners such hostility against himself, so that you may not grow weary or fainthearted. (RSV)

We return to this passage because it so concisely summarizes the author's great hope. Taking all that nourishes us from the Old Testament's "cloud of witnesses," let us run with perseverance. Perseverance, endurance, fidelity has been the homilist's constant exhortation. Endurance is our response to Jesus' endurance on our behalf. We have not yet resisted sin to the point of blood (12:4), even to the point of the shame which Jesus endured. Our hero ran the race, throwing off temptation, ridicule, shame because his eyes were fixed on the joy of complete union with God. In response (and that is what a biblical spirituality means) let us strip down, keep our eyes fixed on Jesus, and move!

The Sacrifice of Jesus

A major function of a priest in the ancient world was to offer sacrifice, to mediate between the gods/goddesses and the participants in any given religion. We have already seen that our compassionate and faithful high priest lives to make intercession on our behalf. He also saves, consecrates and makes us holy. How does Jesus save and sanctify?

Jesus is mediator (8:6, 9:15, 12:24). Today we call in mediators to settle disputes between labor and management, when other kinds of grievances need to be rectified, when warring countries or couples can't seem to speak coherently to each other. There is the possibility, even in today's society, that one of the two parties may be guilty and one innocent. The innocent party would want to hire a mediator who would be credible to the guilty or unjust or offending party. The purpose of mediation would be to break down barriers, to restore communication, to effect reconciliation. The innocent party, God, sent Jesus to us, guilty and hostile as we are, Jesus, credible to us because he is one of us, to mediate.

The exalted Christ, our high priest, mediates a better covenant, a new and lasting covenant (8:6) which makes the first covenant obsolete (8:13). This new covenant is the promise of God's unconditional love. Our minds and hearts are transformed, not because we keep the Law, but because God is merciful (8:10-12) and because Jesus is our reconciler once and for all. There will be no further covenant because he bore the sins of many once for all (9:28).

9:11-15

11But when Christ appeared as a high priest of the good things that have come, then through the greater and more perfect tent (not made with hands, that is, not of this creation) 12he entered once for all into the Holy Place, taking not the blood of goats and calves but his own blood, thus securing an eternal redemption. 13For if the sprinkling of defiled persons with the blood of goats and bulls and with the ashes of a heifer sanctifies for the purification of the flesh, 14how much more shall the blood of Christ, who through the eternal Spirit offered himself without blemish to God, purify your conscience from dead works to serve the living God?

15Therefore he is the mediator of a new covenant, so that those who are called may receive the promised eternal inheritance, since a death has occurred which redeems them from the transgressions under the first covenant. (RSV)

Jesus mediates a better covenant because he uses his own blood, not animal blood; because he enters the real sanctuary, heaven, rather than an earthly tabernacle; because he frees us from sin, not ritual impurity.[4] We may not wince at the idea of a heavenly sanctuary or a covenant in which God offers us unconditional love and forgiveness (offers, not forces upon us; we still need to receive it, to respond to such love). But Jesus' taking his own blood to God for our redemption, Jesus' bloody sacrifice?! How ghoulish, bizarre, even cruel! A modern commentator on this passage, Reginald Fuller, reinforces our horror: "The will of God for Christ was precisely that he should die as a sacrificial victim."[5]

Most of us grew up believing that sacrifice was something difficult, painful, something to make us "bleed a little." We still use the word that way in common parlance: our government sacrifices funds for the poor to build up arms; parents sacrifice for children, etc. Literally, however, to sacrifice is to make holy, to consecrate. Cain's sacrifice was an offering of grains and fruits; later Israelites continued grain offerings and also offered "sacrifices of praise." Yet there is the strong Jewish tradition of holocaust (complete destruction of an animal) or the sprinkling with animal blood as described here in *Hebrews*.

First, we must realize that our use of the word "redemption," buying back, could imply that God has to be paid off by the bloody death of Jesus. Not so. Redemption is much more associated with the deliverance from slavery which God effected in the Exodus. God redeems the Jews from slavery; Jesus redeems us from sin and death.

[4]Fuller, p. 14.

[5]*Ibid.*

Secondly, if as our author instructs us, Jesus is the exact representation of God, then we can know what God wills by observing what Jesus wills in the gospel. Gospel story after story shows Jesus' hatred of pain, misery, blindness, illness, death; shows Jesus' expending every bit of energy to combat people's "victimhood." If Jesus works against death then surely God does not desire Jesus' death as victim.

Next we must understand the significance of blood to the Jews and to the early Christians who were still steeped in Jewish spirituality. Blood was not a sign of death or victimhood. It was a sign of life. The slaying of an animal for sacrifice was not the focus. The slaying was only to release the life. The life, symbolized by blood, was offered as a sign of the offerer's own blood or life. It is perfectly possible that when the disciples of Jesus saw how this innocent man who only went about doing good (Acts 10:38) was slaughtered, their minds leapt to the slaughter of the unblemished lamb which began their exodus pilgrimage to freedom. By the blood of the Passover lamb they were saved as Jews from slavery. By the blood of the Lamb of God they were saved as Christians from sin. God did not passionately desire Jesus' death, but did passionately desire that we should know and accept God's unconditional love, God's fidelity to us, even in our sin, God's freeing activity on our behalf. When Jesus gave his life to drive home that good news, it led to his death, to the release of and offering to God on our behalf all that Jesus was and wanted. The sacrifice, the making holy, was God's response to Jesus' offering of his whole life, including his death. God made Jesus holy, exalted him as Son and great High Priest!

The sacrifice, for the author of *Hebrews*, is more than the death of Jesus. It is one single event which includes the death-exaltation-offering. This sacrifice is, like the exalted Christ himself, "the same yesterday, today and forever" (13:8). His once-for-all offering cannot be repeated.[6] *Hebrews* makes no mention of Eucharist. Yet this book of the New Testament perhaps more than any other calls us to a grateful response of liturgical worship under the leadership of our compassionate faithful high priest.

Community Worship

As we learned in our study of *James* and *I Peter* the spirituality of the first Christians was a communal spirituality. Thus we would expect the author of *Hebrews* to stress the community's response to Jesus' sacrifice. The response of a discerning obedience may be possible for an individual but the response of liturgical worship is necessarily communal and public.

Liturgy comes from a Greek word which means public work, public service. Since service also means ministry in Greek, in this homily the angels are said to minister (1:14). Jesus too ministers, offers public service. Liturgy soon became

[6]McKenzie, "Priest" in *Dictionary of the Bible*, p. 692. This may be difficult for Roman Catholics to understand. Using platonic philosophical categories, we say that Jesus' death/exaltation/sacrificial self-offering is going on continually in heaven. Our Eucharist joins us with Jesus' heavenly sacrifice. In Jewish spirituality, using those categories, we can also say that to remember is to make present again. We celebrate Eucharist in memory of Christ, and so Christ and his self-offering is present again. Eucharist does not repeat Jesus' sacrifice. Thus the nationality or sex of the Eucharistic leader is not important. Only Jesus is "priest" at Eucharist.

associated with public worship (1:7, 8:2, 9:21, 10:11). Perhaps
the recipients of *Hebrews* are withdrawing from liturgical
assemblies (10:25). This would be disturbing to our author
who understands, like the author of *I Peter*, that as a priestly
people we are called to liturgy.

In 7:19, according to Monsignor Myles Bourke, a well
respected commentator on the New Testament's ideas of
priesthood, the phrase "draw near to God," is a Jewish
keyword connoting priestly service.

> Here the Christian life is described in priestly terms; what the
> Old Testament reserved to the priesthood is attributed to all the
> people.[7]

For a priestly people, all of life is worship. The blood of
Christ will "purify our consciences from dead works to serve
(worship) the living God" (9:14). The whole of *Hebrews*
argues that we have been converted from a law, ritual, series of
sacrifices which did not work, which could not really break
through the barriers which our sin had erected. Through the
once-for-all unique sacrifice (death/exaltation/offering) of
Jesus we are freed from that futility in order to worship with
Christ, in Christ, through Christ.

12:28–29 and 13:15–16

> [28]Therefore let us be grateful for receiving a kingdom that
> cannot be shaken, and thus let us offer to God acceptable
> worship, with reverence and awe; [29]for our God is a consuming
> fire.
>
> [15]Through him then let us continually offer up a sacrifice of
> praise to God, that is, the fruit of lips that acknowledge his

[7]Myles Bourke, "The Epistle to the Hebrews" in *The Jerome Biblical Commentary*, 61:41, Englewood Cliffs, NJ: Prentice-Hall, 1968, p. 394.

name. ¹⁶Do not neglect to do good and to share what you have, for such sacrifices are pleasing to God. (RSV)

Christ's is the only sacrifice. We, however, as priestly people can offer our lives. Specifically we can worship with awe and reverence by receiving God's kingdom (12:28). We can also worship together with a sacrifice of praise (13:15) and a sacrifice (a making holy) of doing good and sharing (13:16) with our community.

Obedience Through Discernment

Christ alone can offer the total obedience that God asks. This homily celebrates his obedience. To obey is to listen to, to hear what God wants. To discern what God wants we must know God in the Hebrew meaning of know: be deeply united with; we must be open to what God wants; we must want God's will.[8] Our homilist tells us quite explicitly what God wills for us:

> This will was for us to be made holy by the offering once and for all of the body of Jesus Christ (10:10).

The offering of Jesus' body has already made us holy . Will we accept this, God's will for us?

4:11 — 5:2

> ¹¹Let us strive to enter that rest, that no one fall by the same sort of disobedience. ¹²For the word of God is living and active, sharper than any two-edged sword, piercing to the division of

[8]Thomas Green, SJ, *Weeds Among the Wheat*, Notre Dame, IN: Ave Maria, 1984, p. 63.

soul and spirit, of joints and marrow, and discerning the thoughts and intentions of the heart. [13]And before him no creature is hidden, but all are open and laid bare to the eyes of him with whom we have to do. [14]Since then we have a great high priest who has passed through the heavens, Jesus, the Son of God, let us hold fast to our confession. [15]For we have not a high priest who is unable to sympathize with our weaknesses, but one who in every respect has been tempted as we are, yet without sin. [16]Let us then with confidence draw near to the throne of grace, that we may receive mercy and find grace to help in time of need. (RSV)

5 Indeed, every Jewish high priest, chosen from human beings, is appointed on behalf of human beings with respect to things of God so that the priest might present gifts and sacrifices for sins. [2]He is capable of dealing gently with the ignorant and misled, since he too is surrounded by weakness.

Jesus is our pioneer in a discerning obedience. If the Jewish high priest, described at the end of this selection, can deal gently with a people who are ignorant and wayward (5:2), how much more can Jesus sympathize with our ignorance (lack of discernment) and with our waywardness (lack of obedience). He was tempted as we are (4:15). For Jesus to be tempted means that he had to discern God's voice among the competing voices of his own desires, other people's hopes, even Satan's hungers. For Jesus to be led by the holy spirit means that he was capable of being misled by the evil spirit. That is temptation. Like us, Jesus had to know God intimately, want what God desired, try to stay open to hear God's desire for him. How did he do that?

Our passage moves from "disobedience" (4:11) to a hymn

to the Word of God (4:12-13). All of *Hebrews* would indicate that a privileged place to discover and to grow in knowing God and God's will is scripture. For example, our author quotes extensively from Jer 31:31-34 which promises the new covenant. One feature of that "better covenant" is that each of us will be gifted with an interior sense, through knowing God, of what is pleasing to God. If you are working to be freed from others' expectations of you and "pleasing God" seems like another self-annihilating expectation, substitute "what gives God joy," "what delights God," for "what pleases God." Jesus surely pondered the Word of God in his heart, discovering his Father and what his Father wanted for the poor and the outcast. Jesus responded with his life of ministry and continued discerning day by day, right up to Gethsemane.

The Word of God in scripture is a living Word (Dt 32:47) which does what it says (Is 55:10-11). If we read about God's love and fidelity, we are at that moment receiving it. If we read about God's feeding with manna (Ex 16:14-18), we are nourished; about God's disappointment with David (II Sam 12:1-12), we are scolded; about God's bearing our burdens (Ps 68:19), we are relieved. When Jesus read and listened to the scriptures, he knew they were living, addressed to him, in his time, in his town. He believed that the Word was effective in his life, and responded to it.

The Word comforts us but also, like a sword, penetrates through our darknesses, hiding places, denials of reality and even truth. This word literally "judges the thoughts and intentions of the heart." The word for "judge" is *kritikos*, critical, from which "crisis" is derived as well. Crisis time means a time for judgment, for decision. The Word opens up the secret motives of our hearts so that knowing the truth, we may choose more freely. It was to the Word of God that the evangelists show Jesus turning during his desert temptations and at other decisive times in his life. Jesus was devoted to truth, and the truth of the living, active Word of God made him free in his decisions for God.

5:11-14

> [11]About this we have much to say which is hard to explain, since you have become dull of hearing. [12]For though by this time you ought to be teachers, you need some one to teach you again the first principles of God's word. You need milk, not solid food; [13]for every one who lives on milk is unskilled in the word of righteousness, for he is a child. [14]But solid food is for the mature, for those who have their faculties trained by practice to distinguish good from evil.

"Dull of hearing" would be this author's phrase for disobedience. Disobedience also means lack of faith (3:18-19). God's Word has become unintelligible to these readers. They are, literally, "without experience of the Word of righteousness" (5:13). By contrast, those who would have experience of the Word are those whose faculties are exercised through "practice to distinguish good from evil" (5:14). It is even a greater gift to learn to distinguish between two goods, to discern what would please God more.

10:32-36

> [32]But recall the former days when, after you were enlightened, you endured a hard struggle with sufferings, [33]sometimes being publicly exposed to abuse and affliction, and sometimes being partners with those so treated. [34]For you had compassion

on the prisoners, and you joyfully accepted the plundering of your property, since you knew that you yourselves had a better possession and an abiding one. [35]Therefore do not throw away your confidence, which has a great reward. [36]For you have need of endurance, so that you may do the will of God and receive what is promised. (RSV)

For this author, our acceptance of salvation is understood as enlightenment. In his book on discernment, Thomas Green writes of three qualities one needs to discern: humility, charity and courage.[9] Humility is certainly a fruit of enlightenment when the Word has cut through our mixed motives, our posturings, our denial of our limits, our fallibilities. To know and love and be truthful about ourselves as creatures, God's loved sinners, is humility.

This passage speaks of the readers' humiliation as well, not as something a Christian should seek (though some of us may have been trained in such spirituality). "Being publicly exposed to abuse and affliction" brought these readers into solidarity with each other, led them to compassion (suffering with) and eventual joy.

Their compassion or charity could develop even deeper endurance and courage. The author urges, don't throw away your confidence, don't let endurance wither, for "you need it to do the will of God" (10:36).

13:20-21

[20]Now may the God of peace who brought again from the dead our Lord Jesus, the great shepherd of the sheep, by the blood of the eternal covenant, [21]equip you with everything good

[9]*Ibid.*, pp. 66-67.

that you may do his will, working in you that which is pleasing
in his sight, through Jesus Christ; to whom be glory for ever and
ever. Amen. (RSV)

A discerning obedience is not a virtue which we acquire
and practice but a gift from God. It results in peace: "In God's
will is our peace." Our homilist prays, "May the God of
peace . . ." who is also the God of power "adjust" you in every
good thing. God makes the adjustments (the literal translation
of "equip"), and it is God who works the will of God within
us, through Jesus.

12:5-11

[5]You have forgotten the scripture text which addresses you as
children:

> My child, do not think lightly of the Lord's discipline. Do
> not lose courage when God corrects you. [6]For the Lord
> disciplines those whom God loves, chastises every child
> whom God claims.

[7]Endure this as discipline. God is treating you as beloved
children. What child is not disciplined by a parent? [8]If you do
not receive discipline, which all children share, you must be
illegitimate and not true children. [9]Our earthly parents disciplined us and we respected them. Why not submit even more
readily to our Father of spirits and live? [10]They disciplined for a
short time according to their discretion, but God disciplines us
for our good that we may share the very holiness of God. [11]At
the moment all discipline seems painful but it does yield the
peaceful harvest of justice to all who are so trained.

Peace is the special fruit of a discerning obedience. This
whole passage, which follows the hymn of our Pioneer and
Perfecter's obedience, is about God's disciplining us. Disci-

pline may be out of favor in some studies of spirituality, but again, if we uncover its root meaning we find a richness, not harshness.

Discipline can be seen as disciple-making activity. A disciple is, from its Latin origin, *discipulus/a*, one who learns, a pupil, a student. When we see the emphasis (5:8) which this author puts on Jesus' learning obedience (hearing God), we see that an underlying image of Jesus might be "disciple of the Father." [10] Learning implies openness and eagerness to know, prerequisites for discerning God's desire.

We note a unique title for God in 12:9: "Father of the spirits." Often we hear of "discernment of spirits," one of the spiritual exercises propounded by Ignatius Loyola. Thomas Green explains the gift and the process, and following Ignatius, he invites us to look at the movements of our hearts which Ignatius calls consolation and desolation. God is a God of consolation but Ignatius warns us that at times God purifies us by allowing desolation. *Hebrews* could be in direct dialogue with this sixteenth century Spaniard. Note especially the last verse in the passage quoted above.

> At the moment all discipline seems to be not of joy (consolation) but of grief (desolation); yet later on discipline yields the peaceful fruit of righteousness to those who have been exercised. (12:11)

Long before Ignatius, Jesus offered a criterion for discerning spirits: "By their fruits you will know them." Our peace, our righteousness is the fruit of the Holy Spirit, a sign of our discipleship. So is, according to *Hebrews*, our "work and the

[10]McDonnell, p. 98.

love of his name manifested in serving the saints" (6:10). The criterion for the discernment of the Holy Spirit active in the community is the work, the love, the service of the community in the name of Christ. According to Thomas Green, discernment is "the meeting point of prayer and action." [11]

Summary

Steeped in the Word of God, contemplating the scripture, learning and discerning, the author of *Hebrews* has led us to fix our eyes on Jesus, to respond to his sacrifice by offering our own lives in hope-filled obedience. Let us join our author in praying with the Word of God.

● Return to the questions with which this chapter opened and pray with them now, after your study of the spirituality of *Hebrews*. How has this expression of biblical spirituality deepened your own? How has the Spirit been working in you? Respond to the Spirit with your feelings and hopes.

● Use your imagination to enter the sanctuary of heaven. Jesus is seated in glory at God's right hand, making intercession for you. He strokes God's face and tells God all that he wants for you. Listen to his feelings and hopes for you. Respond now to Jesus.

● Jesus invites you to intercede with him for your family and friends. He invites you very, very close to God. What will you ask God for? You and Jesus are so united it is as though you too are bathed in his glory ("In your light, we are bathed in light" Psalm 36:9, *New English Bible*). Jesus breathes out

[11]Green, p. 50.

peace, love and joy and you breathe it in. Now breathe the peace, love and joy of Jesus onto, into those you love.

● Jesus is our pioneeer. Pioneers take risks. He is like us in every way. The risks we take he has undoubtedly taken: choosing a way of life, separating from his parents, starting his own home in Capernaeum, working at a second career, etc. Remember a risk you have taken. Did Jesus ever experience anything similar? Remember his experience and discuss it with him. For example, I moved out to the ocean, to blocks of solitude, while writing this book. I was afraid of loneliness but risked it. Jesus often risked loneliness and that comforts me. He understands.

● After some decision you make today, reflect on your feelings. Is this decision leading you to greater freedom, peace, love, joy, service? What did you learn about yourself in making the decision? What did you learn about God? Pray not to deny truth when you are making choices. Ask to learn what would delight God.

● Jesus was tempted, just as we are. Can you name four or five temptations you experienced in the past few days? Remember them, whether you succeeded or failed in your struggle. Then ask Jesus to show you where in his living and dying he may have been tempted as you have been. After each memory, beg him: "Your will be done . . . Deliver us from evil."

JUDE AND II PETER

JUDE AND II PETER

● When you were a child, how did you learn the scriptures? What stories did you know and love best? Why? Where did you learn these stories? From whom?

● What was your reaction when you heard about the Jonestown, Guyana mass suicide under the leadership of James Jones? How did you feel about Jones? About his followers? Did you know that they were Christians? If you had been granted "an audience" with Jones a few days before the incident what would you have said, done to deter him? Would it have been easier to speak to the people? How would you have warned them?

● What do you believe will be the future of our planet? Do you believe the image which the New Testament presents of Jesus' returning on the clouds? Will fire destroy the earth? Will it be announced by angels' trumpets? What *do* you believe?

Introduction

These two brief letters are perhaps the least studied, undoubtedly the least prayed in the New Testament corpus.

Jude is only twenty-five verses long, most of it so full of obscure references to Jewish literature current in the first century that it is difficult to relate his words to our contemporary experience. *II Peter*, while claiming to be a follow-up on *I Peter*, written by the apostle himself, is in fact pseudonymous, that is, written by someone else in Peter's name, and heavily borrows from the briefer *Jude*.

Jude is a polemical writing, one which excoriates false teachers and defends the faith, by then come to mean in the development of doctrine, a body of truths and traditions handed down from the apostles. Jude, the author, calls himself a servant of Jesus Christ, and a brother of James. Whoever he is, he is not that one of the Twelve sometimes called Jude Thaddeus. This letter is dated too late for "Jude" to be related to the first Christian generation; it was written between A.D. 90-110,[1] although we don't know from where or to whom. Because Jude relies so heavily on examples from Jewish apocryphal writings, non-biblical writings which nevertheless have biblical content, language and style, most scholars believe he was addressing a Jewish Christian community which could be familiar with those books. For example, some of Jude's sources are *The Assumption of Moses, The Book of Enoch,* and the *Testament of the Twelve Patriarchs.* These apocryphal books were later judged as not divinely inspired by the Jewish rabbis and so were kept out of the canon of the Jewish Scripties, our Old Testament. Yet in Jude's day the rabbis had not yet fixed the canon and therefore many more writings circulated. Jude draws from these. *Jude* itself was not allowed into the canon of the New Testament easily and was only accepted in the fourth century.

[1]Kugelman, p. 76.

II Peter is also polemical, condemning false teachers and especially bolstering that aspect of "the faith" which deals with the end of the world. The author also designates himself a servant of Jesus Christ and an apostle. He links himself to the letter, *I Peter,* and also to its purported author, Peter the apostle who, according to the synoptic gospels, witnessed Jesus' transfiguration on Mount Tabor (II Peter 1:17-18). It seems this author is a more Hellenistic Jew than Jude, on whose writing he also depends. "Peter" is probably writing for gentile Christians of the Hellenistic cultural world, recent converts (2:18). Again, we have no idea from where he writes or what community he addresses, although most scholars suggest that this is a follow-up letter to the communities in Asia Minor addressed by *I Peter.* It is probably the latest of New Testament books, written perhaps even as late as A.D. 140, when heretical teachers preyed upon vulnerable communities.

Knowing now that *Jude* is a dire warning to communities about the dangerous false teachers who are leading them not only into a false understanding but into a sinful way of life, remembering the contemporary Jonestown "massacre" under such demonic leadership, read *Jude's* twenty-five verses through in one sitting and try to feel with our author. As we study the spirituality of these two authors under the rubric of the fullness and the future, the power and the presence, I will basically refer to *II Peter,* so do acquaint yourself with *Jude* before we begin.

The Fullness, the Power

In *Hebrews* we noted how deeply its author was immersed in the Jewish scriptures, how the power of the Word of God energized the "today" of Christians. Another key theme in *Hebrews* is the promise. God's promise is brought to fulfillment in Jesus and his saving work. It is that fullness of God's promise to our ancestors, a promise recorded again and again in scripture, that power of God's promising word to which we turn for deeper understanding in these late writings of the New Testament, *Jude* and *II Peter*.

II Peter 1:12-21

> [12]Therefore I intend always to remind you of these things, though you know them and are established in the truth that you have. [13]I think it right, as long as I am in this body, to arouse you by way of reminder, [14]since I know that the putting off of my body will be soon, as our Lord Jesus Christ showed me. [15]And I will see to it that after my departure you may be able at any time to recall these things.

> [16]For we did not follow cleverly devised myths when we made known to you the power and coming of our Lord Jesus Christ, but we were eyewitnesses of his majesty. [17]For when he received honor and glory from God the Father and the voice was borne to him by the Majestic Glory, "This is my beloved Son, with whom I am well pleased," [18]we heard this voice borne from heaven, for we were with him on the holy mountain. [19]And we have the prophetic word made more sure. You will do well to pay attention to this as to a lamp shining in a dark place, until the day dawns and the morning star rises in your hearts. [20]First of all you must understand this, that no prophecy of scripture is a matter of one's own interpretation. (RSV)

Verse 21 should read, as we conclude this passage: "Not by human willing was prophecy ever delivered, but it has been delivered by human beings speaking by means of the Holy Spirit, speaking from God." Notice in this passage, too, a retelling of the transfiguration story, a sign of Christ's majesty, of his power and presence.

One of the themes of the Jewish scriptures is the importance of memory. For the Israelites, to forget God was to sin. To remember God was to be united with God; to remember God's saving work was to make that salvation present again in the community. "Peter" thus wants to remind his readers of the "present truth" although they do know it already and have indeed been confirmed in that truth. His letter, even after he dies (literally puts off his tabernacle, a word meaning body; perhaps chosen to counteract his opponents who seem to be advocating sexual license), will continue to remind them of their salvation. To forget baptism and its forgiveness of sin means blindness (1:9). Yet his readers are called to light, the light of Christ's transfiguration in glory, the light of the prophetic word.

Peter invites his readers and us to pay attention to that Word. We have already seen in *I Peter* how "paying attention" to the Word can mean our contemplation of scripture, even developing a contemplative attitude with which we can discover God at work in various events, with which we can hear God's word in various circumstances. We have already learned in *Hebrews* how paying attention, "heeding" the Word can mean a discerning obedience.

The Word is a lamp shining in a dark place, literally a "murky" place. The rest of the verse implies that the murky place is the human heart. We remember *Hebrews'* two-edged sword of a Word which lays bare our heart, *I Peter* which reminds us that we are called from darkness into God's glorious light, *James* in which God is named Father of Lights. "Your word is a lamp," the psalmist writes, and Peter concurs.

The light of the Word derives from the Holy Spirit, the Spirit of the risen Christ who is the morning star, who rises in our hearts. The only source of God's word of prophecy is the Spirit. The only way in which the Word can be received as the Word is by the power of the Spirit. We need to be inspired even when we read scripture. To read scripture, to pray scripture is the Spirit's gift. Thus there can be no private interpretation, no claiming truth for oneself, no arrogant boast of knowledge. Absorbing scripture is the Spirit's gift.

"Only those who are animated by the Holy Spirit can give a genuine interpretation of God's Word. This is not an argument against personal reading and reflection on scripture."[2]

Many of us may still be wary of personal scripture study because of Peter's warning against "private interpretation." Hopefully, some of that fear is breaking down. Vatican II assured us how very difficult it is to be "private" in this church-community of ours. Reading, praying with scripture is never a solitary action, although no one may be physically present in the room with us. Because of our renewed understanding of ourselves as community we are always reading as church, praying as church for the church. It is not for our private devotion and growth in holiness that we study and pray the scriptures. The Word of God cannot be chained in, reined in to our private spiritual world.

We could learn from Peter, however, that the more we read, reflect, and share scripture in community the less danger there is that private dreamings or other delusions of absolute truth will carry us away. Not to avoid danger only but

[2]Senior, p. 116.

especially to be enriched by each others' interpretations, we are called to share our pondering of the Word.

Peter pondered the word in his heart. Sometimes the word was difficult to understand, he admits, referring to some of Paul's letters (3:15-16). Sometimes it needed to be pruned of fantastic images, such as those which Jude used. Sometimes, in order to communicate the word to a new audience, biblical images would have to be reworked by Peter into Greek philosophical categories that would be more intelligible to his gentile readers. For example, in 2:4 he consigns the wicked to Tartarus, the Greco-Roman name for the underworld, which our translators simply term "hell."

Peter was quite free with his reinterpretation of Jude. For example, Peter deliberately changed the meaning of Jude's term "glorious ones," Jude was referring to good angels but Peter to the fallen angels. Peter deliberately changed the word "love feasts" of *Jude* 12 to "deceptions" (II Pet 2:13) by playing with similar Greek letters in the two words. Instead of the mythical language of the apocryphal literature which Jude used, Peter avoided "myths" of that sort (1:16), yet used the fire and water cycle of destruction prevalent in Hellenistic mythology.[3] With his scholarly, philosophical vocabularly, he undoubtedly communicated well with his Hellenistic readers but continued the movement expressed in later New Testament writings away from a biblical spirituality to a philosophically oriented spirituality. Peter offered a new hermeneutic to the church of his day.

Pope John XXIII called Vatican II so that our church of

---

[3]*Ibid.*, p. 133.

today could offer a new hermeneutic to the world. Hermeneutic simply means the interpretation of a text, here, a scriptural text. The pope reminded us that we had beautiful and deeply true ancient teachings which no longer communicated to workers, women, the poor, the non-western peoples. We must learn to recast our doctrine in contemporary language which would communicate the good news of salvation. And so John called a Council.

Sometimes, to communicate to a scientifically sophisticated world, we need to de-mythologize parts of the Scriptures.[4] Peter writes: "We did not follow cleverly devised myths when we made known to you the power and presence (coming) of our Lord Jesus Christ" (1:16). Yet, as we will see, Peter clothes the events of Christ's final coming in the mythical language of fiery destruction. Much of our scripture, both Old and New Testaments, is expressed in mythical language. Myth is a universal way of expressing deep and communal truths so that future generations can participate in them. For example, if we speak of the Exodus myth we are not saying that the Exodus is not true, not historical. We are saying that the experience of the people in the presence of mystery was so powerful that they had to create stories and sing songs, use images and archetypal memories to show how the mystery whom they named God freed them from slavery and covenanted with them. The Israelites were not interested in chronicling a factual account of events but wanted to hand on the experience of God in such a way that future generations of Jews in remembering the myth, could re-live the liberation and desert experience of their ancestors with God.

[4]Dermot Lane, *The Experience of God*, New York: Paulist, 1981, p. 23.

Thus myth is very sacred in a biblical spirituality. Yet mythical language, angels and demons fighting over Moses' body, for example, often seems crude and incredible to many of today's sincere believers. If we de-mythologize the language, we must find new and communicating language. We must re-mythologize. How can we, as John XXIII urged, take the core of the myth and retell the story in less fantastic, more credible categories for the various cultures of today's world? That is what evangelization must be about. That was what Peter was about in this "second" letter.

Peter showed such freedom with the scriptures because he knew the Spirit continued to inspire the community and its leaders. The Spirit still continues to reveal the Word in new times, new places. That is why Roman Catholics point to two sources of God's revelation: not only scripture, but tradition, the recurring re-interpretation of scripture generation after generation. Sometimes Christians, including Roman Catholics, get stuck in the literal word or words of a scriptural text and think that God's absolute truth is found in that literal word, or that single verse. That is a simple definition of fundamentalism. Yet as we have seen in *James, I Peter, Hebrews, Jude* and especially in *II Peter*, the early Christians knew that the Word was living, active, changing, meaning one thing to one, another to another. St. Augustine wrote at the end of the fifth century:

> When someone says: "Moses meant what I think," and someone else says: "No, he meant what I think," would it not be more reverent to say: "Why not as you both think, if what each of you thinks is true?" And if in these words someone should see a third or a fourth truth, or indeed any other truth at all, why should we not believe that all these truths were seen by Moses,

through whom the one God tempered the Holy Scriptures to the minds of many, so that their minds should see different things, though all true things.[5]

Peter in this letter can be our model in our own fresh interpretation of scripture for our time.

II Peter 1:1-4

1 Simeon Peter, a servant and apostle of Jesus Christ,
To those who have obtained a faith of equal standing with ours in the righteousness of our God and Savior Jesus Christ:
[2]May grace and peace be multiplied to you in the knowledge of God and of Jesus our Lord.
[3]God's power has given us everything which is full of life and godliness through knowing God completely. God has called us to God's own glory, to God's own excellence. [4]We were given precious and powerful promises by God so that through these promises, you might become sharers in God's own being and escape from lust which corrupts the world.

Peter, like many other New Testament authors, encourages knowledge, but he often uses the single Greek word which means full knowledge. He prays that his readers have full knowledge of Jesus our God and Lord (1:1-2); of the one who called us to his own glory and excellence (1:3); of our Lord Jesus Christ (1:8); and of the Lord and Savior (2:20). Full knowledge of Christ, he writes, does multiply, or make full within us, grace and peace (1:2). It seems that through full knowledge of Jesus these Christians have obtained an "equally precious" faith.

---

[5]Augustine, *The Confessions of St. Augustine, Book 12*, Rex Warner, trans., New York: New American Library, 1963, p. 313.

Most commentators believe that both Jude and this later Peter have equated Christian faith with doctrine, "divinely revealed truths." Donald Senior insists, however, that faith, while losing some of its Pauline connotations of trust, even in these late writings still implies a commitment of the whole person to Jesus Christ.[6] So much of *II Peter*, even this small section, is phrased in Hellenistic categories: divine power, godliness, excellence, divine nature. Yet the great Greek ideal of knowledge is still drenched in the Hebrew meaning of knowledge as personal union, "not simply abstract knowledge of God, but a deep awareness of God through Jesus . . ."[7]

Through our knowing him, Jesus has shared his own divine power (*dynamis*) and called us to his own glory and excellence, that we might become partakers of (literally to be in community with, communion with) the divine nature. Knowledge of Jesus for this author still means a transforming "dynamic relationship with Christ."[8] Peter begins his letter with this joyous reminder of how full knowledge brings full union, and concludes his letter with a prayer that his readers "grow in the grace and knowledge of our Lord and Savior Jesus Christ" (3:18).

II Peter 2:10-22

> [10]and especially those who indulge in the lust of defiling passion and despise authority.
>
> Bold and wilful, they are not afraid to revile the glorious ones,

[6]Senior, pp. 105, 128.

[7]*Ibid.*, 107.

[8]*Ibid.*, p. 111.

11whereas angels, though greater in might and power, do not pronounce a reviling judgment upon them before the Lord. 12But these, like irrational animals, creatures of instinct, born to be caught and killed, reveling in matters of which they are ignorant, will be destroyed in the same destruction with them, 13suffering wrong for their wrongdoing. They count it pleasure to revel in the daytime. They are blots and blemishes, reveling in their dissipation, carousing with you. 14They have eyes full of adultery, insatiable for sin. They entice unsteady souls. They have hearts trained in greed. Accursed children! 15Forsaking the right way they have gone astray; they have followed the way of Balaam, the son of Beor, who loved gain from wrongdoing, 16but was rebuked for his own transgression; a dumb ass spoke with human voice and restrained the prophet's madness.

17These are waterless springs and mists driven by a storm; for them the nether gloom of darkness has been reserved. 18For, uttering loud boasts of folly, they entice with licentious passions of the flesh ones who have barely escaped from those who live in error. 19They promise them freedom, but they themselves are slaves of corruption; for whatever overcomes, to that one is enslaved. 20For if, after they have escaped the defilements of the world through the knowledge of our Lord and Savior Jesus Christ, they are again entangled in them and overpowered, the last state has become worse for them than the first. 21For it would have been better for them never to have known the way of righteousness than after knowing it to turn back from the holy commandment delivered to them. 22It has happened to them according to the true proverb, The dog turns back to his own vomit, and the sow is washed only to wallow in the mire. (RSV)

Most of *II Peter* is directed however against those who do not have true knowledge of Jesus. Knowledge/union means a "way of truth" (2:2), that is, conduct which is faithful to the knowing. In *Jude* the false teachers are primarily described as immoral, but here Peter's opponents preach both wrong doctrine and wrong conduct. Granted, both these letters are polemical and the literary form of polemical writing in that day called for exaggerated accusations of promiscuity, greed, ignorance, etc.[9] In polemics too, there is no logical arguing, just denunciation. The only way to argue with those falsifiers who sneak into the community (2:1) is to live uprightly.

II Peter 1:5-11

> [5]Try with all your heart to supplement your faith with virtue, and virtue with knowledge, [6]and knowledge with self-control, and self-control with steadfastness, and steadfastness with godliness, [7]and godliness with friendship, and friendship with love.
>
> [8]These gifts are abounding in you and so you are not barren or unfruitful in knowing our Lord, Jesus Christ. [9]If, however, you lack these things, you are blind, short-sighted, forgetful that you were cleansed from sin in the past.
>
> [10]Brothers and sisters, be eager to make your calling and your choice firm. Doing this, you will never fail. [11]Instead you will be richly equipped for entrance into the everlasting kingdom of our Lord, our Savior, Jesus Christ.

Peter exhorts his readers to lead a godly life. As sharers of the divine nature by faith (1:4) they are called to respond to God's fulfillment of the "precious and very great promises" (1:4), to his gift-giving divine power (1:3). In Peter's listing of virtue, however, we see the influence of Stoic philosophy which was so to affect our Christian morality and spirituality

---

[9]Gerhard Krodel, "The Letter of Jude," *Hebrews, James, 1 and 2 Peter, Jude, Revelation*. Proclamation Commentaries, Philadelphia: Fortress, 1977, p. 92.

for the next nineteen hundred years. Christians began to strive for virtue, equate morality with self-control, and focus their spiritual growth on winning God's favor rather than responding to God's favor already lavished.

Not only does Peter urge his readers to respond to God's lavishness, but teaches that their "lives of holiness and godliness" will hasten the "day of God" (3:11-12). The major heresy propagated by these false teachers is that the parousia, the glorious coming of Jesus to establish God's kingdom, will never occur. Peter writes to assure the communities that the "day of judgment and destruction of ungodly people" will indeed come (3:7).

The Future, The Presence

II Peter 3:8-10

> 8But do not ignore this one fact, beloved, that with the Lord one day is as a thousand years, and a thousand years as one day. 9The Lord is not slow about his promise as some count slowness, but is forbearing toward you, not wishing that any should perish, but that all should reach repentance. 10But the day of the Lord will come like a thief, and then the heavens will pass away with a loud noise, and the elements will be dissolved with fire, and the earth and the works that are upon it will be burned up. (RSV)

II Peter 3:11-18

> 11Since the whole universe will be dissolved, consider what kind of people you should be, what holy and dedicated lives you should live. 12Wait eagerly for the approaching Day of God and hasten it. The heavens will blaze and pass away, the elements

will melt in flames. ¹³But according to God's promise we can
look forward to new heavens and a new earth in which justice
will find a home.

¹⁴Therefore, beloved, since you do look forward, try with all
your heart to be unblemished and at peace in the sight of God.
¹⁵Remember that the Lord's patience is our salvation. In the
same way Paul, our friend and brother, wrote to you with
inspired wisdom; ¹⁶so he does in all his letters. They *are* hard to
understand. The ignorant and unstable misinterpret them des-
tructively, as they do the other scriptures. ¹⁷You, beloved
friends, know this beforehand. Be careful lest you be carried
away by unprincipled people and lose your balance. ¹⁸Grow in
grace and in knowledge of our Lord and Savior, Jesus Christ. To
him be glory now and forever. Amen.

Jesus' whole mission was to proclaim the kingdom of God,
the new time when God's justice and love and peace would
reign. Jesus' ministry of teaching and healing heralded the
coming rule of God. After his resurrection, the proclaimer
became the proclaimed: Jesus was worshipped as Lord and
Savior, and his kingdom was eagerly awaited. His glorious
presence, or coming, is *parousia* in Greek.

Perhaps nothing so characterizes New Testament spirituality as the longing for Jesus' return in glory to establish the
kingdom of God. When God raised Jesus from the dead, his
followers believed that the end time had already begun and
would soon be consummated in the parousia. The fullness and
the future, the power and the presence of the Lord were now.
By the time *Jude* was written, Christians had begun to cope
with the delay of the parousia. By the time of *II Peter*, Christian
teachers were denying that it would ever occur (3:3-4). Peter
responds to their scoffing by reminding his readers of the
Lord's patience.

It may be hard for us to understand how deeply the early Christians desired the end of the world, even if it were to be destroyed by fire as Peter assumes. This kind of belief is apocalyptic, that is, an inbreaking of God's judgment on an evil and oppressive society. Some New Testament authors assured the early communities that the parousia had already happened, that Jesus, Lord, had established the rule of God in the human heart and in the Christian community. This is called a realized eschatology, a vision of the world's destiny which says we and all creation are already under God's dominion because of Jesus' exaltation. The kingdom, heaven, judgment are already realized, made real. But not completely. Most New Testament thinkers combine their realized eschatology with a belief in a future, definitive return of the risen Lord to claim his own. This could be called apocalyptic eschatology.

Apokalypsis in Greek means the drawing back of a veil, a revelation. Jesus' full and definitive Lordship will be revealed at the end of the world. Apocalyptic literature drew contrasting pictures of horror and glory. For the evil oppressors of Jews (they had numerous apocalyptic writings) and Christians, the end time would be painful, terrorizing. For the ones who longed for God's kingdom, this sudden breaking in of God's reign would be vindication; they would be marked as God's own and rescued from the destruction around them. Noah's rescue serves as the prime model (2:5).

Peter's description of the fiery end would thus be welcomed by his readers. Christian apocalyptic was meant to comfort in times of persecution. Moreover, he transmits a promise of a new heaven and a new earth for the just, one heralded by Isaiah (65:17, 66:22) long ago. This is the "king-

dom of Christ" (1:11), a rare term in the New Testament
which usually points to the kingdom of God. In agreement
with other New Testament authors, Peter envisions this
parousia not only in cosmic terms, but in the personal and
transforming presence of Christ within the believer: "pay
attention to this (the promise of Jesus' total glory manifested
in his transfiguration) ... until the day dawns and the
morning star rises in your hearts" (1:19).

In our days, living under the threat of nuclear holocaust,
Peter's examples of Noah, or Lot saved from the fate of Sodom
and Gomorrah (2:7-8), are not too comforting. We may have
real difficulty in hoping for the coming of God's kingdom if
the world is to be destroyed by fire. Perhaps we are sickened at
our own human responsibility for fiery destructions in the
past and possibly in the future. We know that no one will be
magically rescued from a nuclear disaster. Our children dread
this perhaps even more than we. How can we re-mythologize
the New Testament's apocalyptic hope in God's future?

One way is to touch more deeply into the realization that
the kingdom of God is already within us and among us, that
"the morning stars rises" in our hearts right now. Our growth
in holiness, as Peter teaches, is fostering that rule of God on
earth right now (3:11). If we cannot sincerely desire the
destruction of the old heaven and earth by fire, we can
fervently pray "thy kingdom come" and long for the new
heaven and new earth in which Jesus will be acknowledged as
Lord. We are fairly aware of our individual mortality, our
"private" entrance into the eternal kingdom of Christ (1:11)
at death, but the apocalyptic hope of the New Testament
community serves to remind us of the destiny of all peoples,
the future of the galaxies, the goal of all creation.

Jude 20-24

> [20]But you, beloved, build yourselves up on your most holy faith; pray in the Holy Spirit; [21]keep yourselves in the love of God; wait for the mercy of our Lord Jesus Christ unto eternal life. [22]And convince some, who doubt; [23]save some, by snatching them out of the fire; on some have mercy with fear, hating even the garment spotted by the flesh.
>
> [24]Now to him who is able to keep you from falling and to present you without blemish before the presence of his glory with rejoicing, . . . (RSV)

To conclude this chapter we turn at last to *Jude*. In the Greek of verses 20 and 21 we have one imperative verb: "keep yourselves in the love of God." The other three verbs are participles describing how we are to do that. "Build yourselves up in your most holy faith." For Jude faith means our initial commitment to Christ, but also the tradition that has been handed on by the apostles, the gospel. To build ourselves up in faith today, it would seem appropriate to study the gospels, pray with the scriptures, share our insight about the meaning of the Word and the movements of our hearts as that Word gradually transforms us. This kind of faithsharing in families or small groups would undoubtedly prove a vital help to keeping ourselves in the love of God.

Next we are to "pray in the Holy Spirit." Some Christians would discard the later New Testament writings as too strange and too structured to be of service in contemporary spiritual living. Indeed, as the first communities multiplied, structure did become more necessary. Yet, here, we get a clue that the charismatic was never quenched. Prayer is no formality or obligation but a movement of the Spirit. Some of Jude's opponents may have opposed such prayer. For example, in the

Gnostic Gospel of Thomas we read "If you pray you will be condemned." [10] Praying in the Spirit, for Jude, was a way to stay rooted in the love of God.

The third way to remain in the love of God is to "wait for the mercy of our Lord Jesus Christ" as an immediate experience of his acceptance and a future expectation "unto eternal life." Jude continues by enlisting his readers in the battle against licentious living preached by the Christian heretics. He concludes with a glorious, joyful, hopeful doxology, a brief hymn of praise. Let us pray it with him, using my own translation:

Jude 24-25

> [24]Now to the one powerful to guard you from stumbling, to the one able to set you without blemish, set you rejoicing before God's own glory, [25]to the only God our Savior through our Lord Jesus Christ be glory and greatness, power and authority through all ages, Amen.

[10]Frederick Danker, "The Second Letter of Peter," *Hebrews, James, 1 and 2 Peter, Jude, Revelation.* Proclamation Commentaries, Philadelphia: Fortress, 1977, p. 97.

CONCLUSION

Like seagulls swooping for nuggets of nourishment, we have been fed by certain sections of these five "catholic epistles." There is more to do. I have shared chapters, verses, themes that have meant much to me. Now I challenge you to read through each of these books slowly, asking the Spirit to lead you to what will nourish in a unique, personal way your own biblical spirituality. When memories or images or current experiences in your own life are lit up by a verse or an exhortation or a praise of God, stop reading and let your heart move you toward God. Stay with the feeling or praise or memory as long as it keeps you aware of, attentive to, loving, desiring, asking, or thanking God. Then return to the biblical text until the next word of scripture connects you with God again. If you feel your response to God is weak or distracted or unfeeling, keep reading slowly, perhaps out loud, for even to read scripture is to pray, to be united with God. Trust the Spirit to deepen your biblical spirituality.[1]

[1]McDonnell, p. 10.

Through our study of these five texts we have uncovered some elements of a biblical spirituality. *James* taught us a major biblical principle, a foundation stone of all spiritual life and growth: God takes the initiative in our relationship. It is God who calls us and graces us to be receptive to all that God wants to lavish on us. That lavishing, or blessing, gifts us to respond with single-mindedness, patience, discernment, humility. All these gifts, with our own receptivity, fashion us as wise.

A second major biblical principle is that our spirituality is formed and transformed in community. So we learned from *James* about communal relationships, especially those between the rich and the poor, based on a justice received from God. Compassion and prayer lead us to strengthened community relationships by our "speaking the truth in love."

James is primarily noted as the New Testament work which promotes a faith which flows into action on behalf of the other. It is true that God is the initiator and nurturer of all spirituality, but faith is our response. We learned how we can respond in faith because God is faithful first and calls us to a connaturality, a sharing of God's own values and desires for the world.

I Peter highlighted other aspects of a New Testament spirituality: contemplation; a sharing in the dying and rising of Jesus, such a fundamental gift flowing from baptism; hope in action; and the following of Christ. Contemplation as we learned from this New Testament book, is not wordless nor without content, but biblical contemplation offers us a new vision, a call to move outside ourselves. Instead of passivity in the presence of God, this biblical contemplation is a passionate encounter with God.

Undoubtedly one of the most central elements of a New

Testament spirituality is our relationship with Jesus. Jesus, known particularly in his saving activity of dying and rising, calls us to participate in this dynamic through baptism. Although I Peter uses ransom language to explain the death of Jesus, we re-explored some common notions — and fears — of atonement, blood, and obedience. We examined some images of Christ: Lamb, Servant, rejected stone. We learned how Jesus, more than just offering us a model of suffering, empowers us to die (to sin) and to rise (to justice), to share his sufferings, to make meaning of our own suffering, even to discover joy in suffering.

Baptism has initiated us into the dying and rising of Christ and in identifying us with the risen Christ has offered us a new identity. With Christ, we are a new family, a chosen race, a royal people, a community of priests, a holy nation, the very household of God. Baptism has transformed us, making us with Christ prophets, priests, and royal-born. With this new and power-filled identity, we the baptized are missioned to tell good news, to be signs of hope, to witness to the world.

I Peter has promised us energy and life in abundance, both signs of hope. As a new creation through baptism we are neither passive in our hoping nor merely optimistic. In James it was faith that was expressed in action. Hope too expresses itself in action, we learned from this author. Some specific ways in which Christians witness to the world are by providing for the poor and homeless; by our godly behavior which attracts the godless to our God; by breaking the cycle of violence; by participating in and influencing every human institution.

Finally we noted the pilgrim images found in I Peter and attended to Jesus as our leader in pilgrimage. We heard our author urge: "Come to him," and we learned that the perfection of our faith, our salvation depends on his faithful leadership.

We began our study of *Hebrews* by circling back to two themes of *I Peter*, two aspects of a biblical spirituality: hope grounded in God's word and Jesus himself. Then we specifically focused on Jesus' initiative in this relationship which is our spirituality, an initiative symbolized in his sacrifice. Our multifaceted response to Jesus' whole-hearted initiative was narrowed to two aspects about which the author of *Hebrews* can instruct us. Both are important elements of a biblical spirituality: community worship and obedience through discernment.

If our hope in the future is based on God's word, then we look to scripture, the record of God's action on our behalf in the past. From the Jewish scriptures the Christian community learned to trust God's past fidelity; from their own experience of Jesus they learned to trust God's fidelity into the future, because Jesus runs into God's future. Their hope, our hope is a gift given in community and for the sake of community. A major theme of *Hebrews* is that Jesus is our better hope. Hope gives confidence, faith means endurance, and both are centered on our doing the will of God.

Jesus comes to do the will of God, to learn obedience, our author has taught us. The very Word of God and exalted Son, superior to every leader and lord and even the angels, tasted death on our behalf. He, flesh and blood brother to us, was brought to perfection by God through his sufferings and through his obedience in the midst of physical pain and emotional abandonment. Tempted like us, yet without ever rebelling against God, he is our compassionate high priest who spends his new life in God's presence interceding for us.

We re-examined common notions of Jesus' bloody sacrifice. We learned that our loving God could not passionately desire Jesus' agony and death. Instead, God wanted Jesus' holiness and wants our own. God hates evil and the suffering it engenders. So God sent us Jesus to war with demons and death, sickness, pain and victimhood. Thus the author of *Hebrews* rightly views sacrifice as making holy, views blood as a sign of life-union. More than death, this author has assured us, the sacrifice of Jesus also includes his exaltation and offering of himself.

In communal worship we activate our baptismal identity as priests. We offer Jesus in his dying and rising. His sacrifice makes our entire lives holy, this author has written, so that all Christian life is worship.

Besides our worship, another core response to Jesus' sacrifice on our behalf which this author has highlighted is our obedience. A biblical spirituality fosters the discernment which makes obedience anything but conformity; rather, it is a free and flexible response to the Word of God in any and every situation. It is the Word of God according to *Hebrews* which probes and lights and sifts the motives and spirits of our hearts.

God's promise which permeates the Jewish scriptures finds its fullness in the New Testament. *II Peter* described the fullness and the power of that promise. The author uses the image of light, relying on the Spirit for interpretation of the scriptures. They do need interpretation as we try to make sense of some of the other fantastic images which this author and the author of *Jude* used. The author of *II Peter* himself has offered a new interpretation of the scriptures to a community becoming more philosophically oriented. Thus we learned something about hermeneutic and why evangelization is so central to the mission of today's church.

Like almost every book of the early church, *II Peter* stressed "full knowledge" of Jesus. However, the author also taught a stoic morality. By our holiness, he continued, we can hasten the glorious coming of Christ.

Like almost every New Testament book, too, both *II Peter* and *Jude* looked forward to the parousia, the apocalyptic breaking in upon us of God's future. For them, the wicked would be destroyed, but their own Christian communities would be welcomed into the new heaven and the new earth. The hope that sturdily grows when surrounded by the possibilities of fiery destruction is our Christian heritage in an age of nuclear threat.

I opened these chapters with a very simple definition of biblical spirituality: our relationship with the God who reveals and offers God's very self, not only in the pages of scripture but in the person of Jesus and in the ongoing influence of the Spirit in our day-to-day living. Hopefully, through our dialogue with the five authors of the "catholic epistles" and their communities, we are more alert and attentive to the Word taking flesh in our lives and in our communities.

One of the best ways to let the Spirit deepen your biblical spirituality is carefully and especially prayerfully to read the scriptures and to ponder them in your heart. Mary undoubtedly had a most profound and most enlivening biblical spirituality. She heard the word of God, contemplated it, let it be done to her, and acted on it. To encounter the living and active Word of God is such an adventure! So, "with our eyes fixed on on Jesus, let us run . . ."

SUBJECT INDEX

BIBLICAL INDEX

New Testament